HOW WE STOPPED
LOVING
THE BOMB

Other books by Douglas Roche

The Catholic Revolution (1968)
Man to Man (with Bishop Remi De Roo, 1969)
It's a New World (1970)
Justice Not Charity: A New Global Ethic for Canada (1976)
The Human Side of Politics (1976)
What Development Is All About: China, Indonesia, Bangladesh (1979)
Politicians for Peace (1983)
United Nations: Divided World (1984)
Building Global Security: Agenda for the 1990's (1989)
In the Eye of the Catholic Storm (with Bishop Remi De Roo and
Mary Jo Leddy, 1992)
A Bargain for Humanity: Global Security By 2000 (1993)
*Safe Passage into the Twenty-First Century: The United Nations' Quest for
Peace, Equality, Justice and Development* (with Robert Muller, 1995)
An Unacceptable Risk: Nuclear Weapons in a Volatile World (1995)
The Ultimate Evil: The Fight to Ban Nuclear Weapons (1997)
Bread Not Bombs: A Political Agenda for Social Justice (1999)
The Human Right to Peace (2003)
Beyond Hiroshima (2005)
Global Conscience (2007)
Creative Dissent: A Politician's Struggle for Peace (2008)

HOW WE STOPPED
LOVING
THE BOMB

AN INSIDER'S ACCOUNT OF
THE WORLD ON THE BRINK
OF BANNING NUCLEAR ARMS

DOUGLAS ROCHE
WITH A FOREWORD BY ROMÉO DALLAIRE

JAMES LORIMER & COMPANY LTD., PUBLISHERS
TORONTO

James Lorimer & Company Ltd., Publishers acknowledges the support of the Ontario Arts Council. We acknowledge the financial support of the Government of Canada through the Canada Book Fund for our publishing activities. We acknowledge the support of the Canada Council for the Arts which last year invested $20.1 million in writing and publishing throughout Canada. We acknowledge the Government of Ontario through the Ontario Media Development Corporation's Ontario Book Initiative.

Cover design: Meghan Collins
Cover image: iStockphoto

Library and Archives Canada Cataloguing in Publication

Roche, Douglas, 1929-
        How we stopped loving the bomb : an insider's account of the world on the brink of banning nuclear arms / Douglas Roche.

Includes bibliographical references and index.
Issued also in electronic format.
ISBN 978-1-55277-652-0

        1. Nuclear disarmament. 2. Antinuclear movement. I. Title.

JZ5675.R59 2011   327.1'747   C2010-907787-3

James Lorimer & Company Ltd., Publishers
317 Adelaide Street West, Suite 1002
Toronto, ON, Canada
M5V 1P9
www.lorimer.ca

Printed and bound in Canada
Manufactured by Friesens Corporation in Altona, Manitoba, Canada in February 2011.

*For my grandchildren
Isabelle, Nicholas, and Cesar.
May they live in a world free of nuclear weapons.*

CONTENTS

FOREWORD

WHEN I THINK OF THE LONG-FOUGHT BATTLE TO BAN NUCLEAR WEAPONS, MY mind inevitably drifts to my grandchildren and the legacy we are leaving the post–Cold War generation. As the Honourable Douglas Roche points out, this is a bright and vibrant generation with enormous potential to reach beyond the limits of what previously seemed possible. I am reminded of a speech I once gave at a high school just south of Winnipeg. After I spoke, a Grade 11 student asked me: "Why are we worried about plastic bags and dirty water when we have the ability to completely obliterate and eliminate the whole of the environment, the whole surface of the earth?" I was left speechless. Indeed, we are sending very mixed messages to our youth. *How We Stopped Loving the Bomb* challenges us to lead by example and bridge this chasm between our indifference and the unconscionable, destructive potential of nuclear weapons.

Nuclear weapons, by their very nature, threaten human rights around the globe. We need to take the opportunities that are given to us and do everything in our power to ensure that the world is safer for future generations. It is time for us to start thinking seriously about how Canada can help move forward the discussions on the abolition of nuclear arms. Canada should be clearly associated with the resolution of these challenges to world peace and prosperity and universally known as an advocate for a nuclear disarmament.

We need to ask ourselves: Does Canada really believe in this? If so, how can we use our resources to ensure that future generations will live in a world without nuclear weapons? If we really believe in abolishing nuclear weapons—and I think we do—then we have to prove it. Canada has extensive and unique experience directly relevant to preventing nuclear proliferation. Shouldn't we make the most of that expertise and put those skills to use? One area in which Canada could make a significant and invaluable contribution is verification. Nearly every initiative outlining the necessary steps for nuclear disarmament stresses the need for an effective system of verification. The key element of such a system will be unrestricted access to nuclear weapons facilities by inspectors.

Canada has a proud history of leading the field of verification research for arms control and disarmament. By bringing together the very best experts in government, the academic community, and the private sector, Canada has been able to develop important technological, legal, and institutional tools of verification. We can rightly claim that these tools constituted a significant contribution to the international framework upon which the watershed arms control agreements in Europe in the 1980s were negotiated and implemented.

My point is not to dwell on past initiatives or past accolades, although it is worth noting that the Verification Research Program operated successfully on an annual budget of only $1 million. Rather, I want to draw attention to Canada's demonstrated ability to respond to the needs of the international community in the practical and meaningful way that we have done in the past. This is the kind of thinking we need now. We need this country's leadership. We need this country's best minds to take on this role. Verification is only one issue central to the disarmament objective. Achievement of this objective will require the dedicated effort of countries like Canada to promote transparency, act as an honest broker, and put all the required multilateral processes into action.

Public indifference is driven mostly, I think, by a deep skepticism that a global ban on nuclear weapons is actually possible. To be honest, sometimes I find myself sinking into that same skepticism. Canadians have a great national narrative based on our global values in support of justice and proaction, yet lately our record runs completely contrary to this. Years of diplomatic efforts and tireless civil society campaigning, though encouraging, have not had the effect that we could rightfully hope for. In the meantime, the situation seems to be getting worse. Not only are nuclear weapons firmly entrenched in the mindset of powerful politicians and individuals, but a growing number of unscrupulous individuals have also come to see them as a means to assert themselves on the global stage.

In the face of such difficulty, I admire Senator Roche's courage in writing this book and I am deeply grateful because it provides both the inspiration and the tools to take up the cause. It is my hope that *How We Stopped Loving the Bomb* will serve to initiate a debate in our country and draw attention to an issue with which Canada could and should be more actively engaged. There is growing momentum behind the global campaign to ban nuclear weapons. We need to seize this historic opportunity and do everything in our power to ensure that the world is safer for future generations.

I sincerely hope we are ready to respond to this call for action.

Lieutenant-General the Honourable Roméo A. Dallaire, OC, CMM, GOC, MSC, CD, (Retired), Senator

INTRODUCTION

SHORTLY AFTER I WAS ELECTED TO PARLIAMENT IN 1972, I STARTED REGULARLY visiting the United Nations in New York, concentrating on international development as a basis for peace. I journeyed through China, Indonesia, and Bangladesh to examine various models of development.

Then, in 1978, an event occurred that widened my perspective. The UN convened for the first time a special session on disarmament, the largest and most representative meeting of nations ever held to consider the issues involved in lowering the level of armaments everywhere. The meeting's Final Document called nuclear weapons "the greatest danger to [humanity] and to the survival of civilization," and suggested nations start a comprehensive, phased program with agreed time frames leading to the complete elimination of nuclear weapons "at the earliest possible time." Until then, nuclear disarmament had not been a significant public issue, but this UN special session had a galvanizing effect on the peace movement. Freezing the development of new nuclear weapons became a popular cause.

As the 1980s started, the Cold War was coming to its peak, with about sixty-five thousand nuclear weapons in existence, most many times more powerful than the bombs that destroyed Hiroshima and Nagasaki. The UN convened a second special session on disarmament in 1982. Two days before it opened, one million people marched in New York from the UN building to Central Park to protest the never-ending accumulation of arms. The United States and the Soviet Union held the lion's share of nuclear weapons, but the three other permanent members of the Security Council—the United Kingdom, France, and China—were also building up their stocks. By this time, I was president of Parliamentarians for Global Action, an international body of parliamentarians devoted to building a more peaceful world. I was given the opportunity to make a ten-minute speech to the session from the General Assembly podium. "Despite the many lofty speeches made from this platform," I said, "the world is running out of patience and time…We condemn the continued arms race as a crime against God and humanity." The meeting ended with no advances, the delegates barely able to reaffirm the Final Document of the previous session.

When the third special session on disarmament was held in 1988, I had become Canada's Ambassador for Disarmament and led the Canadian delegation to the meeting. The hard realities of international politics bore down on me. The Western nations considered it realistic to support steps toward nuclear disarmament, such as reductions in the numbers held by the US and the Soviet Union, but unrealistic to call for immediate negotiations to shut down the development and deployment of all nuclear weapons. Rajiv Gandhi, then the Prime Minister of India, came to the podium to propose a fifteen-year plan to eliminate all nuclear weapons in phased stages. The Western states gave him the backs of their hands.

Any suggestion that questioned the core doctrine of nuclear deterrence was immediately attacked. Under nuclear deterrence, states justified their possession of nuclear weapons on the grounds that the weapons were meant to deter nuclear attacks and thus had to be maintained and even modernized, even while their overall number was being reduced. Though all the nuclear powers had signed the Nuclear Non-Proliferation Treaty, which called for all parties to pursue negotiations in good faith toward nuclear disarmament, they resolutely refused to enter a process of comprehensive negotiations. What this amounted to was the big states' maintaining their nuclear arsenals, while pretending to disarm. More and more, I could see the accuracy of Swedish Nobel Peace Laureate Alva Myrdal's book, *The Game of Disarmament,* which describes how states move their pawns around the disarmament chessboard. The nuclear arms race was becoming institutionalized, not ended.

That year, I became chairman of the UN Disarmament Committee and travelled to the nuclear power capitals—Moscow, Washington, London, Paris, and Beijing—as well as to the Conference on Disarmament in Geneva. I asked for meaningful progress on nuclear disarmament resolutions. At the beginning of the committee's first deliberations in New York, I established an open-ended "Friends of the Chair," as an informal group of ambassadors to advise me, and drew attention to two recent studies showing in great detail the environmental and economic impact of the ever-growing accumulation of weapons. Resolutions piled up. When it was over, I was thanked for my efforts. The game went on.

In 1989, the Berlin Wall fell and, for a moment, it looked as though "a new world order" might be established with the Cold War being relegated to the past. The US and the Soviet Union, now Russia, made significant cuts in their nuclear weapons. The general public, confident that reduced numbers meant freedom from the threat of Armageddon, relaxed; and the nuclear issue disappeared from sight. But the old world disorder quickly reappeared when Saddam Hussein, the Iraqi dictator, invaded Kuwait; wars broke out in Africa; and Yugoslavia succumbed to competing internal forces. Cuts in nuclear weapons slowed, then stopped. Neither the US nor Russia would go below several thousand each.

The Nuclear Non-Proliferation Treaty (NPT), having been established in 1970 with a twenty-five-year period, came up for review in 1995 and states had to decide what to do with it. Many developing countries accused the nuclear powers of insincerity in building up a two-class world in which they, the rich and powerful, maintained their power through nuclear weapons while proscribing their acquisition by any other state. I attended the month-long meeting and saw how the major players bullied the conference president, Jayantha Dhanapala of Sri Lanka, who was in favour of an extension of the treaty on the condition that it specify time frames for concrete steps leading to the elimination of all nuclear weapons. In the end, the treaty was extended indefinitely, without any conditions.

The treaty came up for review again in 2000. By then I was chairman of the Middle Powers Initiative, a non-governmental organization of nuclear disarmament specialists working closely with some thirty middle-power states. Our meetings were designed to help those states exert leverage, however modest, toward getting the nuclear powers to fulfill their legal obligation to accomplish nuclear disarmament. We collaborated with the New Agenda Coalition, a group of states led by Ireland and Sweden, determined to make progress on the nuclear agenda. The New Agenda did some hard bargaining with the nuclear weapons states and produced a document in which the nuclear powers pledged an "unequivocal undertaking" to total nuclear disarmament via a program of Thirteen Practical Steps. Though no time frames to accomplish this were specified, the review meeting ended jubilantly. The euphoria was premature, however, because the next year President George W. Bush entered the oval office, repudiated US support for the Comprehensive Test Ban Treaty, and did away with the Anti-Ballistic Missile Treaty that had managed to get the US and the Soviet Union to promise not to build missile defences. His administration's attitude to nuclear disarmament virtually eviscerated the Thirteen Practical Steps.

As the Middle Powers Initiative chairman, I attended all the preparatory meetings for the Non-Proliferation Treaty review conference in

2005, and found them a ritualistic facade. Not only was no progress made, but the 2005 meeting even took a step backwards when the US refused to acknowledge the commitments it had made in 1995 and 2000. The meeting ended in deadlock, with Brazil tartly warning, "One cannot worship at the altar of nuclear weapons and raise heresy charges against those who want to join the sect."

I found it astonishing that the meeting could so lightly pass over the warning issued at the outset by UN Secretary-General Kofi Annan. Imagine, just for a minute, he said, the consequences of a nuclear catastrophe on one of the great cities of the world. "Tens, if not hundreds, of thousands of people would perish in an instant, and many more would die from exposure to radiation." Economic, health, food, and transportation systems would collapse. Who would suffer the worst effects? Those who were already poor.

At the Middle Powers Initiative my colleagues and I, dismayed at the fiasco of the 2005 review conference and the major powers' callousness, decided to start a new project, the Article VI Forum, named after the article of the Non-Proliferation Treaty that mandated comprehensive negotiations. We considered the international situation so sour that the most productive work we could do would be to lay the groundwork for the legal, political, and technical requirements for a nuclear-weapons-free world. Thirty invited states participated in four Article VI Forum meetings held at the UN, The Hague, Ottawa, and Vienna. In 2007, I presented our findings to Ambassador Yukiya Amano, chairman of a meeting preparing for the Non-Proliferation Treaty's 2010 review.

That seemed, at the time, the most that international diplomacy could accomplish, especially with the Bush administration still in office. But in 2008, with the election of Barack Obama, the situation changed dramatically. The new president brought to the White House his long-held vision of "a nuclear-free world." Perhaps it was just out of relief that the Bush era was finally over, but Obama's early actions were praised as having world-changing potential, especially with Russia's leaders also proclaiming their desire to eliminate nuclear dangers. A new wave of hope spurred a renewal of advocacy and action to abolish nuclear weapons once and for all.

No sooner had Obama revealed his intentions to steer the world toward the elimination of nuclear weapons, even if it could not be achieved, as he said, in his lifetime, than the nuclear defenders took to the stage, repeating the old falsehoods that security requires the maintenance of nuclear weapons. The nuclear weapons defenders made it clear they intended to stop Obama cold in his quest for a nuclear-weapons-free world, or at least to make the president accept that such a goal could be reached only "eventually," which means so far over the horizon as to be meaningless.

With questions about Obama's real intentions and capability swirling through every chancery in the world, governments prepared for the 2010 Non-Proliferation Treaty review conference. This book begins with the drama surrounding that event.

The title, *How We Stopped Loving the Bomb*, reflects the change in public attitudes to nuclear weapons over the years. In 1964, one of the top movies was *Dr. Strangelove, or: How I Learned to Stop Worrying and Love the Bomb*, starring Peter Sellers. It is a black comedy in which an insane general starts a process leading to nuclear holocaust that a war room of politicians and generals frantically tries to stop. The film, which won four Oscar nominations, is still regarded as political satire of a high order. It seemed to give relief to the public's pent-up fears about nuclear warfare that had been aroused by the 1962 Cuban missile crisis. It made the MAD (Mutually Assured Destruction) doctrine comical. Whatever director Stanley Kubrick's intention may have been, the effect of the film was to relax people, and they forgot about possible catastrophes. But today's documentary films, such as *Countdown to Zero* and *The Tipping Point*, are designed to awaken feelings of revulsion against nuclear weapons and to spur efforts to eliminate them.

The world has stopped loving the bomb—that much progress has been made. The political will to ban all nuclear weapons is gathering. The long love affair will finally end when enough people really do start worrying about what will happen if every middle-sized country gets the bomb.

PART ONE

PUBLIC OPINION VS. DIPLOMATS' DELAYS

1

THE PEOPLE'S HOPES

EARLY SATURDAY EVENING, MAY 1, 2010, WITH CROWDS GATHERING FOR THE usual weekend festivities, a terrorist tried to blow up Times Square in New York, thus exposing modern life once more to the vulnerabilities of a nuclear attack. The police were forced to evacuate thousands of tourists, and I was diverted to a roundabout way back to my hotel after dinner. In one of those juxtapositions that, from time to time, show the world going in two directions at once, Times Square was the scene the next afternoon of a rally of fifteen thousand people, who marched from Broadway along Forty-second Street to the United Nations on First Avenue to protest against nuclear weapons. A failed bomb attack and a peace march, a scare and a hope, the ugly realities of daily life and a vision of a safer future. These discordances collided in my mind as I joined the marchers.

The would-be bomber, arrested two days later, left a crude device made from gasoline, propane, firecrackers, and alarm clocks in a smoking Nissan Pathfinder, which was soon discovered. The ensuing lockdown of Times Square added to the government's fears that another 9/11 terrorist attack on US soil is inevitable. President Obama had been quite explicit three weeks earlier at a summit of forty-seven nations in Washington when he warned that stolen nuclear materials could easily be fashioned into a nuclear weapon: "Just the smallest amount of plutonium—about the size of an apple—could kill and injure hundreds of thousands of innocent people." Terrorist networks such as al-Qaeda are always trying to acquire the material for a nuclear weapon. Such use, the president added, "would be a catastrophe for the world—causing extraordinary loss of life, and striking a major blow to global peace and stability."

There was no sign of disruption when I returned to Times Square to join the marchers the afternoon after the failed bomb attack, though it was easy to spot the plain-clothes security personnel mixed in with the gathering crowd. A Japanese woman approached me and, with a smile, handed me a green paper crane. This has become the universal symbol of Hiroshima, where the first atomic bomb was dropped on August 6, 1945, at 8:15 AM, killing a hundred and forty thousand persons. A few years later, a young girl, Sadako Sasaki, who had been not far from where the bomb exploded, developed leukemia from the atomic radiation and was given only a year to live. Inspired by a Japanese legend that a wish would be granted to anyone who folded a thousand origami cranes, Sadako painstakingly began folding cranes out of any paper material she could find. She died before reaching the thousand, but her schoolmates completed the project for her. Sadako's cranes have become a memorial to all the victims of nuclear warfare. Her spirit lives on in the survivors, known as *hibakusha*, of both the Hiroshima and Nagasaki blasts. I have known many hibakusha, and their message is simple and powerful: "No one else should ever suffer as we did."

A steel-drum band performed on a platform on the side of Seventh Avenue, and it stopped every so often for speeches. One of the first was by the mayor of Hiroshima, Tadatoshi Akiba, whom I first met in 1999, his first year in office. Akiba has become famous as the president of Mayors for Peace, an organization of more than four thousand mayors around the world, which is promoting a campaign to rid the world of nuclear weapons by 2020. Akiba speaks flawless English, the result of his spending twenty years teaching mathematics at the Massachusetts Institute of Technology in Cambridge.

A few speeches later, a slim, red-haired woman in a purple dress came to the microphone and, in a few challenging words, had the crowd ready to march. Jackie Cabasso is at once a fiery activist and a critical analyst who can produce an academic paper with forty-three footnotes. A leading voice for nuclear disarmament for twenty-five years, Cabasso lives in Oakland, California, where she is the executive director of the Western States Legal Foundation, which monitors and challenges the work of the US nuclear weapons laboratories and provides legal support for non-violent protesters. Deeply committed to non-violence, she herself has been arrested many times during non-violent protests against US nuclear weapons. She is tough on the US government: "If the most powerful military force in history insists that it still needs nuclear weapons to defend itself, how can we realistically expect less powerful states to forego them?"

Cabasso has spoken at public hearings, legislative symposia, and conferences around the US and in Europe, Japan, Korea, Russia, Kazakhstan, Polynesia, India, China, and Brazil. In 2009, she was awarded the Sean MacBride Peace Prize, named after a distinguished Irish statesman and former president of the International Peace Bureau. Because Cabasso takes a big-picture approach, it's easy to see why she's so popular. "Nuclear disarmament," she says, "should serve as the leading edge of a global trend toward demilitarization and redirecting resources to meet human needs and restore the environment."

Cabasso was a founding member of the Abolition 2000 Global Network to Eliminate Nuclear Weapons, which has grown to include more than two thousand participating groups in ninety countries, the largest non-governmental anti-nuclear network in the world. As she stepped down from the platform, she was joined by her partner, John Burroughs, a bearded, rumpled-looking lawyer, whose PhD dissertation at the University of California at Berkeley dealt with the international law framework for nuclear weapons policies. Burroughs is executive director of the New York–based Lawyers' Committee on Nuclear Policy, the UN office of the International Association of Lawyers Against Nuclear Arms, which he represented at the 1998 negotiations in Rome for the founding of the International Criminal Court. Burroughs writes the most coherent briefs on nuclear disarmament issues to be found anywhere. Jackie is outgoing, John more studious in demeanour, opposite qualities that may be the root of their attraction for each other. Together, they make a formidable team.

Cabasso, Burroughs, and I started marching along Forty-second Street, recalling the "One Million March" of 1982 when, at the height of the Cold War, close to one million people paraded from the UN to Central Park to protest the deployment of Pershing and cruise nuclear missiles in Europe. That demonstration had affected both US President Ronald Reagan and Mikhail Gorbachev, who would in a few years take the leadership of the Soviet Union. Reagan and Gorbachev signed a treaty to eliminate intermediate-range nuclear missiles and, at Reykjavik in 1986, came within a whisker of an agreement to banish nuclear weapons entirely, until a dispute over a US-planned missile defence system (known at the time as "Star Wars") got in the way and the moment was lost. Nonetheless, the US and Russia did enter into a further agreement to reduce the number of strategic missiles and, after the Berlin Wall suddenly fell in 1989, ending the Cold War and resulting in the dissolution of the Soviet Union, the fear of nuclear war receded from the public mind. That there are still 22,600 nuclear weapons in existence, and that other countries are going nuclear seems lost on the public mind.

Cabasso, Burroughs, and I talked about this decline in "public punch" as we passed Bryant Park and the Public Library on our right and then Grand Central Station on the left. The day's numbers were respectable but nowhere near the 1982 throngs that filled the streets of Manhattan. Fear of nuclear war was the great motivator then; hope for the abolition of nuclear weapons was the common denominator now. We debated hope versus fear as motivating forces for action. Then Cabasso had to hurry ahead because she was to join a group of Japanese peace activists presenting a giant petition at the UN.

Sergio Duarte, an affable and highly experienced Brazilian diplomat, is High Representative of the UN Secretary-General for Disarmament Affairs, an exalted title he wears with modesty and charm. Since the Japanese petitioners could not enter the UN building on a Sunday, Duarte came down to the street to greet them. I have known Duarte since his days as Brazilian Ambassador to Canada. He was president of the Non-Proliferation Treaty review conference in 2005 that turned into such an acrimonious stalemate as a result of the Bush administration's intransigence. Duarte and I stood chatting on the sidewalk while the petitioners gathered. "Don't you think the mood is better this time with Obama in the White House?" I asked him. "Yes," he said, "but it's going to be tough, very tough to get any agreement."

The march ended at Dag Hammarskjöld Plaza on Forty-seventh Street, across from the UN, where booths had been set up with all manner of books, DVDs, posters, and T-shirts. Singers and bands performed, and a general air of festivity prevailed. The lines of police officers had nothing to do.

THE TRAP OF *EVENTUAL*

I went back to the nearby Beekman Tower Hotel to prepare for the guests I had invited that evening to honour Alyn Ware, one of the most industrious figures the nuclear disarmament movement has ever known. Though he is now a grandfather, Ware has a boyish look to him and a very soft manner, which is quite deceptive because he is a master strategist in planning nuclear disarmament campaigns as he travels around the world advising parliamentarians. His work as global coordinator of the seven-hundred-member Parliamentarians for Nuclear Non-Proliferation and Disarmament is only one of his many educational activities for which he won the 2009 Right Livelihood Award. Often called the "Alternative Nobel Prize," the Right Livelihood Award is presented each year in the Swedish parliament "for outstanding vision and work on behalf of our planet and its people." Other winners have included David Suzuki, the Canadian environmentalist, and Tony Clarke and Maude Barlow for their work to promote the fundamental human right to water.

Alyn Ware started out as a kindergarten teacher in New Zealand and developed the Peace Studies Guidelines that became part of the New Zealand school curriculum. His international career blossomed when he coordinated the World Court Project, which achieved, in 1996, a historic ruling from the International Court of Justice on the illegality of nuclear weapons. I brought him with me on many delegations to capitals when I was chairman of the Middle Powers Initiative, an organization sponsored by several prominent nuclear disarmament groups, which encourages key middle-power countries to press for the systematic elimination of nuclear weapons. I wanted this celebration of Alyn's achievements to focus on the future, so I had invited several of our highly informed colleagues, among them highly experienced Ambassador Henrik Salander of Sweden; Ambassador Jayantha Dhanapala of Sri Lanka, former disarmament chief at the UN; David Krieger, president of the Nuclear Age Peace Foundation in California; Rob Green and Kate Dewes, long-time activists from New Zealand; and Jonathan Granoff, president of the Global Security Institute in the US; as well as Burroughs and Cabasso.

For nearly three hours, over a couple of bottles of wine and hors d'oeuvres, we debated whether the "Obama moment," as everyone was calling the US president's expressed vision of moving to a nuclear-weapons-free world, is just a flight of rhetoric or grounded in action. I led off the discussion, arguing that the world is in a trap: if we admit the validity of the word *eventual*, nuclear disarmament is unlikely ever to occur because the spread of nuclear weapons to other countries in the coming decades will reinforce the determination of the major nuclear powers to maintain their arsenals, and gradually the imperative of disarmament will fade away. The moment opened up by Obama must be seized and forced upon the international community now, I argued.

"It's time to be brutally frank," Dhanapala said. His words always carry weight because, in 1995, he presided over the conference that made the Non-Proliferation Treaty permanent. "There is a huge hole in the Obama basket," he said, cautioning us not to put all our hopes in Obama alone. Obama is already moving to the right to stave off attacks from the reactionary elements that drive political discourse in the US, he said. He is forced into the position of trying to salvage his agenda, not be transformational. Therefore, Dhanapala concluded, the only way to get a global ban on nuclear weapons is to press like-minded states to start building the structure now, not wait for the recalcitrant nuclear weapons states to instigate it.

The discussion turned to how much Obama could or should act on his own vision. He did, after all, convene the unprecedented summit of the UN Security Council in September 2009 and the subsequent Washington summit on nuclear security, both of which put an international spotlight on the need to tighten measures to safeguard nuclear materials and to advance non-proliferation and disarmament measures. And he did sign a new agreement with Russia to slightly reduce strategic weapons. On the other hand, David Krieger pointed out, Obama's actual steps are not much more than arms control, rather than nuclear disarmament. He argued that Obama did not seem willing to act on his own vision. "Therefore," Jonathan Granoff argued, "the middle-power states must redefine and act on the abolition issue over the next five years." The energetic discussion ended on the note that, while Obama had opened up space on the international agenda for serious discussions on a nuclear-weapons-free world, we had to move beyond him.

BAN KI-MOON, A CAMPAIGNER

The next morning, May 3, I found my way through a maze of renovation construction materials into the General Assembly Hall of the United

Nations, which is dominated by the giant gold mural hovering over the green ivory podium where virtually every world leader of the past six decades has spoken. As a long-time adviser to the Holy See delegation to the UN, I had credentials to admit me to the current (the eighth) review conference of the Non-Proliferation Treaty. The review conferences are month-long events that happen every five years. The treaty, whose 190 member states comprise the largest arms control and disarmament treaty group in the world, came into existence in 1970. It has three main purposes: to accomplish nuclear disarmament through negotiations, to stop the spread or proliferation of nuclear weapons to other countries, and to facilitate the peaceful use of nuclear energy. Most unschooled media commentators assume that the title of the treaty defines its principal function, thereby omitting the nuclear disarmament pillar. The Non-Proliferation Treaty's famous Article VI says: "Each of the Parties to the Treaty undertakes to pursue negotiations in good faith on effective measures relating to cessation of the nuclear arms race at an early date and to nuclear disarmament, and on a treaty on general and complete disarmament under strict and effective international control." Actually, the treaty was a bargain between the nuclear haves and have-nots. The nuclear weapons states—the US, Russia, the UK, France, and China, who are also the permanent members of the UN Security Council—agreed to pursue negotiations in good faith on nuclear disarmament in return for the non-nuclear weapons states' not acquiring nuclear weapons and being guaranteed access to nuclear technology and materials for peaceful use.

The treaty has neither stopped the spread of nuclear weapons, though it certainly has contained it, nor led the powerful five to close down their nuclear arsenals. Since there are still, two decades after the end of the Cold War, so many nuclear weapons in existence with no comprehensive negotiations in sight, how can the treaty be said to be working? Every review conference, and I have attended six of them, has been filled with charges against the possessors that they are ignoring their legal obligation to negotiate elimination, while the possessors defend themselves by pointing to reductions they have undertaken, adding that security conditions in the world have not ripened to the point where nuclear disarmament is possible. Hence they stick to the "ultimate" goal of "eventual" nuclear disarmament, which the majority of states in the world now claim is just a dodge for permanency.

I watched that morning as the conference delegates went through the formality of electing Libran Cabactulan, a Philippines diplomat who had prepared himself well with consultations around the world, as its president. Cabactulan quickly brought the UN Secretary-General, Ban Ki-moon, to the podium.

When Kofi Annan's second term as Secretary-General expired in 2006, it was Asia's turn to fill the post. The permanent members of the Security Council, who each have veto power over the nomination of any candidate, and thus control the voting, selected the mild-mannered Ban Ki-moon, former foreign minister of South Korea. It is often said that the big five want more of a secretary than a general in the post so as not to have their own power diminished, but, on the nuclear disarmament issue at least, Ban turned out to be a general. Unlike his predecessors, who usually kept the subject of nuclear disarmament at arm's length because any action inevitably stirs up tensions, he has openly campaigned for the end of nuclear weapons.

In 2008, he issued his own five-point plan, which undoubtedly afflicted the powerful. He called for a new convention or set of mutually reinforcing instruments to eliminate nuclear weapons, backed by strong verification; a UN summit on nuclear disarmament; rooting nuclear disarmament in legal obligations; requiring nuclear weapons states to publish information about what they are doing to fulfill their disarmament obligations; and limiting missiles, space weapons, and conventional arms—all steps that are needed for a nuclear-weapons-free world.

Two days before the opening of the 2010 Non-Proliferation Treaty review conference, he gave a rousing speech to several hundred civil-society activists at New York's Riverside Church, where he stated, to cheers: "Nuclear disarmament is not a distant, unattainable dream. It is an urgent necessity, here and now. We are determined to achieve it." Negotiations, he added, "are long overdue," and he put the full weight of his office behind a Nuclear Weapons Convention, which would be a global treaty banning all nuclear weapons.

It doesn't do for a Secretary-General to whip up enthusiasm when speaking to professional diplomats, so Ban Ki-moon was more restrained when he addressed the review conference delegates, but his message was no less pointed. "I challenge you to take the steps today that will set the stage for a breakthrough tomorrow. We need more examples of what can be achieved—not more excuses for why it is not possible."

IRAN VS. THE US

The highlight, or perhaps the low point, of the opening morning of the conference occurred as the President of Iran, Mahmoud Ahmadinejad, gave his speech. Many Muslim speakers, as he did, preface their formal speeches by invoking "the name of God, the Compassionate, the Merciful," which is supposed to put the listener into a high-minded state. "The nuclear bomb is a fire against humanity rather than a weapon for defence," he began. But he descended quickly from elevation when he attacked the US for having used nuclear weapons, and "the Zionist regime," which "consistently threatens the Middle Eastern countries." The reputation of Ahmadinejad, who in the past has frequently denigrated Israel, had preceded him into the hall, so the Western delegates were ready to walk out on his speech when he reached the references to Israel. In twos and threes, they began departing in what was supposed to be a show of rejection.

What the Non-Proliferation Treaty needs is more genuine dialogue, not shouting, so it is unfortunate that the disruption detracted everyone from absorbing Ahmadinejad's eleven proposals, which began with a call for nuclear disarmament "through transparent, binding, and effective mechanisms buttressed with solid international guarantees." The suspicion that Iran, a member of the Non-Proliferation Treaty group, is using its access to nuclear energy to build a nuclear bomb clouds many minds. But Israel, which possesses about eighty nuclear weapons and has not signed the treaty, escapes close scrutiny. Ahmadinejad's rhetoric certainly undermines the credibility of Iran, whose spiritual leaders have decried nuclear ambitions, but the country is standing solidly in support of the 1995 Non-Proliferation Treaty resolution on the establishment of a nuclear-free zone in the Middle East. The future of this contentious issue requires dialogue, not knee-jerk rejection.

After lunch, US Secretary of State Hillary Clinton could be seen sitting in the seats beside the podium, awaiting her turn to speak. She seemed tired and her eyes, when she appeared on the huge TV screens, looked drawn. She clearly commanded the respect of the audience when, after preliminary comments, she said, "Iran will not succeed in its efforts to divert and divide." Iran, she said, was the only country at the conference not fulfilling its nuclear safeguards obligations. Iran has not been fully transparent in opening its nuclear facilities to international inspectors to prove it is not developing a bomb. There was a veiled threat in her comment that the US would not use nuclear weapons against non-nuclear-weapons states that are parties to the NPT and in compliance with their nuclear non-proliferation obligations. However, in calling on Iran to join with other states in fulfilling their common obligation to strengthen the global non-proliferation regime, Clinton seemed to be leaving the door ajar for some diplomacy. She went on to make news with her statement, "Beginning today, the United States will make public the number of nuclear weapons in our stockpile and the number of weapons we have dismantled since 1991."

Within an hour, the Pentagon released a statement that the US had 5,113 warheads in its nuclear stockpile, down 84 per cent from a peak of 31,225 in 1967. The figure includes warheads that are operationally deployed, kept in active reserve, and held in inactive storage. But it does not include several thousand warheads that are now retired and awaiting dismantlement. Left unsaid was why the US needs more than five thousand nuclear weapons, the smallest of which contains explosive power several times the strength of the bomb that destroyed Hiroshima.

A complete picture of nuclear weapons in the world was published in the 2010 yearbook of the Stockholm International Peace Research Institute, the pre-eminent weapons research institute. If all nuclear warheads are counted, including fully operational warheads, spares, those in both active and inactive storage, and intact warheads scheduled for dismantlement, eight states—the US, Russia, the UK, France, China, India, Pakistan, and Israel—together possess a total of more than twenty-two thousand warheads, at 111 sites, in fourteen countries.

NUCLEAR WEAPONS WORLD TOTAL

"Sheer, dumb luck" is the reason that no nuclear weapons have exploded since Hiroshima and Nagasaki, Gareth Evans, former Australian foreign minister, told a noon-time event at the UN for civil-society representatives. Non-Proliferation Treaty conferences are always closely monitored by members of non-governmental organizations, many of them seasoned campaigners who know more about the issues than many of the

COUNTRY	FULLY OPERATIONAL WARHEADS	OTHER WARHEADS	TOTAL
USA	2,468	7,100	9,600
RUSSIA	4,630	7,300	12,000
UK	160	65	225
FRANCE	300	. .	300
CHINA	. .	240	240
INDIA	. .	60 – 80	60 – 80
PAKISTAN	. .	70 – 90	70 – 90
ISRAEL	. .	80	80
TOTAL	7,560	14,900	22,600

diplomats, for whom a period in their government's disarmament office is only a step, if not a pause, in their careers. At this conference, 121 organizations were represented by more than fifteen hundred people, who participated in highly informative seminars on technical subjects.

The committee room was filled to hear Evans and Yoriko Kawaguchi of Japan, co-chairs of the commission established by the governments of Australia and Japan to develop a practical agenda for nuclear disarmament. There has been, in fact, no shortage of prescriptions offered by several international commissions over the years. Each new offering stimulates the process, and the Evans-Kawaguchi report was given a lot of attention. Its central message struck a refrain: "So long as any state has nuclear weapons, others will want them. So long as any such weapons remain, it defies credibility that they will not one day be used, by accident, miscalculation, or design. And any such use would be catastrophic."

Evans defended the report's principal recommendation that the total number of nuclear weapons in the world be reduced to two thousand by the year 2025, which would be 10 per cent of current numbers. Many activists consider this insufficiently ambitious and want a target of zero set now and accomplished within specified time frames. But Evans said achieving a nuclear-weapons-free world will be a long, complex, and formidably difficult process and so a "minimization point" should be emphasized now. When I asked him whether preparatory work on a Nuclear Weapons Convention should start now in parallel with a continuation of steps such as more reductions, the entry-into-force of the Comprehensive Test Ban Treaty, and a new global ban on the production of fissile materials, he allowed that, yes, the Final Document of the treaty review conference should at least have some reference to such a convention.

But that was definitely not how senior members of the US delegation saw things when I spoke to them that evening at Ambassador Cabactulan's reception. Any mention of a Nuclear Weapons Convention, with the implication that the US would have to eliminate all its nuclear weapons, would be stridently opposed by Republican Senator John Kyl of Arizona, one official told me. Kyl's opinion matters because he was the Senate's number-two Republican, and he is considered an expert on nuclear weapons. Kyl consistently demands more money for modernizing US nuclear weapons and opposes US ratification of the test ban treaty. He is, in short, Obama's nuclear nemesis in Congress, and the official I spoke to feared that if the treaty review conference upset Kyl, he would oppose ratification of the new START (Strategic Arms Reduction Treaty) between the US and Russia, which, modest as it is, is considered vital to enabling Obama to do anything more on nuclear disarmament. The Obama team realized they needed Republican support to win the sixty-seven votes needed for Senate consent. When I suggested that Obama can't have it both ways, in raising hopes for a nuclear-weapons-free world and then opposing preparations for a global ban, the official just shrugged. But a colleague intervened: "Listen," he said, "France will never agree to a convention, so the US isn't to blame."

COMPULSORY RETIREMENT AT SIXTY-FIVE

Was Evans right in holding off immediate consideration of a global ban until nuclear weapons reductions are consolidated? I wondered. This could be a politically pragmatic approach, but it presumes "good faith" on the part of the nuclear weapons states. How can they be in "good faith" when they are continually modernizing their arsenals to be just as lethal with fewer numbers? Again, the trap of *eventual* nuclear disarmament.

Mayor Akiba of Hiroshima will have nothing to do with the word *eventual*. The Mayors for Peace campaign wants action to start now on a Nuclear Weapons Convention to enable the world to reach zero nuclear weapons in 2020. On the second day of the conference, Akiba convened a meeting of mayors who had flown to New York to make their case. The featured speaker was no less than the Secretary-General of the UN, who once again called for immediate action. "The UN should be the new Ground Zero for nuclear disarmament," Ban Ki-moon said. When he announced that he would go to Hiroshima for the sixty-fifth anniversary commemoration of the August 6 bombing, and thus be the first Secretary-General to visit Hiroshima, Akiba beamed.

As he always does, Akiba linked the suffering of the hibakusha to the future. One of the reasons 2020 was specified as the target for the end of nuclear weapons, he said, is because 2020 is the natural limit imposed by the average age of the hibakusha, which is now more than seventy-five. "We are duty-bound to abolish nuclear weapons while they are still alive. We do owe it to them, who have shown through their sufferings and sacrifices that nuclear weapons are absolute evil." The year 2020 will also be the fiftieth anniversary of the Non-Proliferation Treaty. If it hasn't achieved its goal of ridding the world of nuclear weapons by then, its effect is very likely to be dissipated in future decades. Akiba has mounted a robust organization, which has reached into 143 countries. He makes the telling point that the municipalities of the world have every right to tell their national politicians to eliminate nuclear weapons, because it is communities at the local level that will be completely devastated by a nuclear blast.

The government speeches piled up during the first week of the review conference with hardly a hint of urgency, let alone passion for the future of humanity. It was as though the governments were competing in abstractions. One pleasant exception was the speech of the Austrian Foreign Minister, Michael Spindelegger, who announced Austria's commitment to establish a "Competence Centre for Nuclear Disarmament and Non-Proliferation" in Vienna, which would work closely with civil society. "Many projects, such as the Mine Ban Treaty or the Convention on Cluster Munitions, would not have turned out as successfully had it not been for the work of dedicated non-governmental organizations," he said. "It is my firm belief that strengthening of the monitoring role of civil society can further our goal of a world free of nuclear weapons."

The conference devoted Friday afternoon of the first week to three hours of presentations by non-governmental organizations' representatives, and it was here that the human scale of the issue broke out of the grey prose of the bureaucrats. Nobel Peace Laureate Jody Williams cast aside her text to make an eloquent call for action now. Rob Green, a former British naval commander with the responsibility for delivering nuclear strikes, skewered the nuclear doctrine that undergirds the retention of nuclear weapons: "The belief in nuclear deterrence is based upon the crazy premise that nuclear war can be made less probable by deploying weapons and doctrines that make it more probable." Jayantha Dhanapala, a former high official himself, took the unusual step of appearing with the humble NGOs. "We do need a radical change," he said. "We need to begin the process of outlawing nuclear weapons."

The speech that impressed me the most was given by two German students, Barbara Streibl and Fatih Oezcan, representing Ban All Nukes generation (BANg), a European youth network for nuclear disarmament founded in 2005. One of BANg's actions was in Büchel, Germany, where twenty US nuclear weapons are deployed as part of the NATO nuclear-sharing arrangement. A couple dozen students showed a Hiroshima-Nagasaki exhibition to soldiers guarding the base and, when they were shooed away, staged a sit-in demonstration resulting in several arrests. Barbara and Fatih took turns speaking: "Our generation was born after the Cold War. We had nothing to do with the creation and proliferation of these weapons. The Cold War is over and humanity is facing new problems. These twenty-first-century problems cannot be solved by twentieth-century weapons. We are young and we have new ideas. We are growing up in a globalized world, where modern communication and technology connects so many of us. Today young people have friends all around the world…We are able to build trust. We do not fear foreign cultures and religions…Nuclear weapons are now sixty-five years old. Don't you think it's time for compulsory retirement?"

With this one speech, the fresh vision and hopes of the new generation tackled the tired clichés of the old. I took some heart in looking at these two fine examples of a generation that may, finally, be able to break from the bonds of the past. Outside the UN, the late afternoon New York traffic was as frenetic as ever as I tried to find a cab to go to the airport and home. New Yorkers don't have time to think about the abstractions of nuclear weapons. Except, of course, when a failed bomber causes Times Square to be locked down.

2

THE DIPLOMATS' DELAYS

WHEN I PASSED THROUGH US IMMIGRATION AT THE TORONTO AIRPORT MAY 25, 2010, on my way back to New York for the final week of the Non-Proliferation Treaty review conference, the American officer asked me the purpose of my journey. "I'm going to the United Nations for a conference on how to get rid of nuclear weapons," I replied. He looked at me quizzically. "Too much testosterone," he said, as he stamped my passport. Nuclear warheads as phallic symbols are probably best left to psychologists, but there is no doubt that nuclear weapons are all about power in the world. The immigration officer may well have summed up in those three words the root of the problem nuclear abolitionists face.

The power of the nuclear weapons states was on display when I rejoined the conference, now in the huge conference rooms in the temporary building on the north lawn of the United Nations while the main building undergoes renovation. The conference had gone through its committee stage with three main committees and subsidiary bodies delving into great detail on the treaty's main pillars: nuclear disarmament, non-proliferation, and peaceful use of nuclear energy. All their reports had been consolidated into a single document called the President's Draft of the Final Document. Ambassador Libran Cabactulan was in the chair, listening attentively as delegates tore the document apart and proposed one amendment after another. The mood was tense and cautious. To speed the process along, Cabactulan interjected, "I think the Chair has heard enough," an admonition that evoked laughter throughout the room. It seemed that the delegates did not want to break the goodwill even as they stuck to their polarized national positions.

Multilateral diplomacy is like a ballet in words, the performers executing minute steps with finesse and grace, except that at the UN they do it in six languages. It takes a pungent phrase every so often to make clear what's really going on. A choice one was offered by Rebecca Johnson, a brilliant analyst and editor of *Disarmament Diplomacy,* who, on her blog, criticized the addiction of the nuclear weapons states to their weaponry. The conference, she said, "can't wait for the alcoholics to vote to close down the brewery." Both the sex and the alcohol metaphors are apt in describing the behaviour of the big states at the session. Like addicts facing withdrawal, they consistently resisted any language in the president's document that would simply get the job of nuclear disarmament done.

Egypt, a nation which has developed itself as a link between the Arab world and Europe, always plays a major role at disarmament and non-proliferation conferences. Its diplomats, though circumspect, aren't afraid to lead in tackling contentious issues. In 1995, it played the pivotal role in securing a Non-Proliferation Treaty resolution calling for the establishment of a Middle East Zone free of weapons of mass destruction. The resolution expressed concern over the continued existence in the Middle East of unprotected nuclear facilities: though not named, Israel was the clear object of concern. At the 2010 conference, Egypt was also leading the Non-Aligned Movement, which had been born during the Cold War as an association of states aligned with neither the West nor the Eastern bloc. It currently numbers 118 states, which habitually express their repudiation of the nuclear weapons states' feeble, if not duplicitous, steps toward nuclear disarmament. For years, the Non-Aligned Movement has called for a time-bound program for the phased elimination of nuclear weapons.

One of Egypt's most experienced ambassadors, Maged A. Abdelaziz, thus found himself in a key position at the conference, and he immediately set out to play a bridging role. On the first Sunday evening, he invited Cabactulan, Duarte, Dhanapala, the representatives of the nuclear weapons states, the chairmen of committees, and the ambassadors of a select group of states, including Germany, Austria, and Iran, to dinner at his residence and a round-table discussion on how to make the conference a success. He repeated the process on two more occasions, and this group evolved into an informal "friends of the chair," guiding Cabactulan. But not even Abdelaziz's camaraderie could break through the nuclear weapons states' opposition to a Nuclear Weapons Convention.

Cabactulan bravely carried forward language from the committee report that a convention would "contribute" to achieving a world without nuclear weapons, even though the idea had been firmly rejected by the US, Russia, the UK, and France. Not even tying the reference to a convention to the Secretary-General's five-point plan would sway them. Russia said advocating for a convention was a "red line" they would not cross. France said it could tolerate the word *convention* only if it was moved out of the action section. The UK didn't want to hear the word at all. The US supported the other three and added, for good measure, that it objected to language calling for the closing of test sites. Only China, which had previously voted in favour of a convention in UN resolutions, gave a tacit consent.

Abdelaziz, seeing that a nuanced approach was going nowhere, weighed into the debate with an amendment that represented the non-aligned states' determination to force the hand of the nuclear weapons states. To an opening statement in the recommendations section that would have the conference agreeing to an action plan for nuclear disarmament, he wanted to add the words, "within a specified framework of time, including a Nuclear Weapons Convention." His nuclear opponents rejected this completely. The conference was clearly heading for the lowest common denominator as the basis for a Final Document—or for outright failure. Though the Non-Proliferation Treaty does allow for voting, its states have always worked through consensus. While voting may give one side a quick victory, a long-range movement of the whole international community, in the view of most diplomats, can be achieved only by general agreement.

On the evening of May 25, Abdelaziz hosted a reception at the Egyptian mission on Forty-fourth Street, near the UN, in honour of his compatriot, Mohamed Shaker, whose three-volume study, *The Nuclear Non-Proliferation Treaty: Origin and Implementation, 1959–1979,* is the definitive work on the subject. Since present-day scholars need the work, which has long been out of print, the Egyptian Council for Foreign Affairs and the James Martin Center for Nonproliferation Studies, Monterey, California, had combined to reissue the book as a compact disc. The party was in honour of this event and Shaker, modest as always, made a gracious speech. I had first met him when he was president of the 1985 review conference and I led the Canadian delegation as Ambassador for Disarmament. The priority that year was getting agreement on language calling for negotiations on a comprehensive test ban to start immediately. When the US balked, a ballet of words began. *Immediately* was diluted to *as a matter of highest priority.* Even that was too much for the US to swallow, so Shaker introduced an ingenious formula by inserting an umbrella paragraph over the final text stating that there was consensus that some delegations believed this and other delegations believed that. The device took the pressure off for the moment, but it only papered over the division between the nuclear powers and the non-aligned movement.

Shaker's book, which developed out of his doctoral thesis, begins with this quotation from the UN's 1978 First Special Session on Disarmament, whose Final Document is often called the "bible" of nuclear disarmament: "It is imperative, as an integral part of the effort to halt and reverse the arms race, to prevent the proliferation of nuclear weapons. The goal of nuclear non-proliferation is on the one hand to prevent the emergence of any additional nuclear weapons states besides the existing five nuclear-weapon states, and on the other progressively to reduce and eventually eliminate nuclear weapons altogether." The core problem identified in this quotation has persisted through the decades. It is the juxtaposition of the words *progressively* and *eventually* that has caused the trouble. *Progressive* is open to several interpretations, but the most likely meaning here is "advancing step-by-step." However, *eventual* refers to something's taking place at an unspecified later time. The nuclear powers put the end of nuclear weapons so far off into the future as to have no meaning in a modern context.

Many observers at the conference think this is precisely what Hillary Clinton had in mind when she closed her speech by saying: "Forty years from now, our successors will mark the eightieth anniversary of the Non-Proliferation Treaty." Why would the treaty be needed four decades from now if its purpose in producing a nuclear-weapons-free world had been achieved? Pentagon spokespersons have indeed talked of the US having nuclear weapons forty years from now. That is why the word *eventual* is a trap.

OFF-THE-RECORD BRIEFINGS

I went around the room at Abdelaziz's reception, meeting longtime friends. Randy Rydell, a senior policy adviser to Ambassador Duarte, was feeling dejected by all the negative comments that had been made about the draft Final Document, which he and an assistant had stayed up all night preparing. Ambassador Alison Kelly of Ireland, who had been entrusted with overseeing an agreement on the contentious Middle East section, was ebullient in anticipated success. Ambassador Alexander

Marschik of Austria, a strong supporter of a Nuclear Weapons Convention, went into some detail with me about Austria's proposed "Competence Centre" and the role of civil society. Already his mind was into the next five-year cycle of work. Tariq Rauf, a Canadian who has become a world leader through his work at the International Atomic Energy Agency, saw the present battle over texts in terms of a last-ditch stand by the nuclear holdouts.

The Treaty's rules permit civil-society representatives to attend plenary meetings but not committee sessions. The major states have always resisted letting the public see how adamant is their resistance to a comprehensive program for nuclear disarmament. The NGO community gets around this by inviting a friendly ambassador each morning to give an off-the-record briefing. The morning after the reception, it was the turn of a well-regarded Western ambassador, who made it clear that the nuclear weapons states were working industriously to weaken the language in the review conference's President's Draft. While Mr. Obama appears more serious about abolition than any of his predecessors, the gap between the Western states and the Non-Aligned Movement is still enormous, he said. The nuclear powers were sticking to incremental steps that did not lead to any comprehensive solution. Yet they wanted a successful outcome of the conference so as to preserve the credibility of the Non-Proliferation Treaty, which, they argue, gives them cover for holding onto their weaponry until *eventual* kicks in. That being said, the ambassador added, the era of nuclear weapons is clearly coming to an end.

The demise will be hastened by creating a humanitarian norm against nuclear weapons, an approach the ambassador commended Switzerland for having introduced into the conference when that country's foreign minister, Micheline Calmy-Rey stated: "As a nuclear war would threaten the very survival of our common humankind, a debate should be launched concerning the legitimacy of the use of nuclear weapons regardless of the legitimacy of the motive of defence that can be invoked...In fact, it is necessary to ask the question, at which point the right of states must yield to the interests of humanity." All this provided solid basis for the argument that work should begin now on a Nuclear Weapons Convention.

Cabactulan, desperate to find bridging language and at least give the convention some official status, which was a key wish of his own Philippine government, sent the delegates back into small sessions behind closed doors; but the parade of amendments and counter-amendments continued. In an extraordinary move for a Secretary-General, Ban Ki-moon intervened with an open letter to all governments appealing for compromise to avert a failed conference. The message was clear: two failed conferences in a row would doom the Non-Proliferation Treaty. But it was also clear that the price of unity was the lowest common denominator, which was precisely what the president's team produced in an amended version of the President's Draft. Cabactulan presented it at 5 PM on May 27, the second to last day, with the comment, "This may not satisfy many, but it may be the answer to our prayers." That would depend, of course, on what you were praying for.

MIDDLE EAST BOILING POINT

Since 1995, a major stumbling block to Non-Proliferation Treaty agreements has been what to do about the Middle East. Though Israel has from its founding in 1948 pursued a nuclear weapons program, the country maintains a "nuclear ambiguity" position by which it neither confirms nor denies that it possesses nuclear weapons. It first built a nuclear weapon in 1967–68 and now has about eighty. Because Israel has rejected the Treaty, Israel's nuclear facilities are not under international safeguards. The nation's clandestine arsenal is not only a thorn in the side of its Arab and Iranian neighbours, but an impediment to the overall Middle East peace efforts, which appear to be an endlessly frustrating process. The antagonism burst out into the open at the 1995 NPT review conference, when Eygpt and its Arab allies threatened to derail the indefinite extension of the Treaty unless the conference addressed the need for a Middle East zone free of weapons of mass destruction. It was a Canadian, Ambassador Chris Westdal, who brokered a compromise between Israel's patron the US and the Arab states. A special resolution drawn up in the midnight hours called on "all states in the Middle East to take practical steps in appropriate forums aimed at making progress towards, *inter alia*, the establishment of an effectively verifiable Middle East zone free of weapons of mass destruction."

In the intervening fifteen years, with no implementation of that resolution, international attention has shifted to Iran, whose nuclear development program has led to suspicions that it is secretly building a nuclear weapon. Iran's co-operation with the International Atomic Energy Agency inspection process has been sporadic, causing the UN Security Council to enforce sanctions. Still, Iran jealously guards its "inalienable right" under Article IV of the Non-Proliferation Treaty to enrich uranium for peaceful purposes.

At the time of the 2010 review conference, a public fight was brewing over an initiative taken by Brazil and Turkey, non-permanent members of the Security Council. Under this plan, Iran had agreed to send 1,200 kilograms of its low-enriched uranium to Turkey, which would act as an intermediary in sending back to Iran higher-enriched nuclear fuel from Russia and France to be used in an Iranian medical research reactor. This would have allayed concerns that Iran was enriching uranium to bomb level, but the deal was scuppered when the US pressed the Security Council into imposing new sanctions on Iran.

For the Arab states, the problem of keeping nuclear weapons out of Iran is resolvable; but not if Israel is given carte blanche. The Arab states want to pinpoint Israel's existing, though not acknowledged, nuclear weapons; the US wants to keep the focus on Iran's putative weapons. So who is really the bad boy of the Middle East, Israel or Iran?

The Non-Aligned came into the 2010 conference demanding action in the form, at least, of a conference of all Middle East states. Cabactulan at the outset hived off the volatile Middle East issue from committee discussion, entrusting it to Alison Kelly, whose Irish charm was a starting point for bringing discordant sides together. The depth of the issue, however, called for hard-headed backroom politics beyond the diplomatic niceties. When the conference reached its last days, the political muscle of US Vice-President Joe Biden was called upon. He gave a dinner for Middle East ambassadors in Washington, where a deal was put together. The language went to President Obama for final approval. Israel would be named, though gently, in the Final Document, and Iran not. But "all states" in the region would be called upon to take relevant steps to achieve a nuclear-weapons-free zone. Thus the section on the Middle East in Cabactulan's document reaffirmed "the importance of Israel's accession to the treaty and the placement of all its nuclear facilities under comprehensive International Atomic Energy Agency safeguards."

The document then got to its key decision: "The U.N. Secretary-General and the co-sponsors of the 1995 Middle East resolution, in consultation with all the states of the region, will convene a conference in 2012, to be attended by all states of the Middle East, on the establishment of a Middle East Zone free of nuclear weapons and all other weapons of mass destruction...and with the full support and engagement of the nuclear weapons states." A facilitator will be appointed to make the conference happen. But will it happen? Israel said immediately that it would not attend, but it is hard to see how its credibility in the prolonged Middle East peace process can be maintained if it does not. The Israel-Iran showdown on nuclear weapons looms.

ACCEPTING THE MINIMUM

It is extremely unlikely that the Middle East imbroglio over nuclear weapons can be resolved by itself. Israel fears being dominated if not invaded by Arab enemies should it ever be deprived of its nuclear deterrent. So it claims that a comprehensive Middle East peace plan is a prerequisite to nuclear disarmament. A comprehensive peace plan is likely unattainable as long as Israel is the sole state in the region to possess nuclear weapons.

More and more, it appears that a global plan to ban all nuclear weapons—everywhere—is the only way to get them out of any one country or region. The Non-Proliferation Treaty is so compromised by forty years of non-action on its key element of comprehensive negotiations for elimination that it cannot achieve a nuclear-weapons-free zone in the Middle East. That is why a Middle East conference of "all states" in the Middle East in 2012 is a good idea, even if the conference is delayed a year or so. If the US is to succeed in its determination to keep nuclear weapons out of Iran, it will have to bring Israel to the table.

Such a Middle East conference, going beyond the Non-Proliferation Treaty, increases the validity of a Nuclear Weapons Convention, which, by bringing India and Pakistan to the table as well, would also reach beyond the existing Treaty's confines. The world is preparing for a truly global framework for all nations to address their joint responsibility to proceed to a nuclear-weapons-free world. President Obama contributed to this enlarged thinking when he invited the leaders of India, Pakistan, and Israel to his Washington summit on nuclear security.

While the Non-Proliferation Treaty has shown that it cannot produce a nuclear-weapons-free world, neither can this goal be achieved with the Treaty in tatters. A scorned NPT would just make the nuclear weapons states dig their heels in harder. Recognition that the failure of the 2010 conference was not a viable option drove the nuclear disarmers to accept the minimum that the nuclear weapons states were willing to offer. On the question of a Nuclear Weapons Convention, the centrepiece of the discussions, Cabactulan was forced to use the softest language possible. His final version said: "The conference notes the Five-Point Proposal for Nuclear Disarmament of the Secretary-General of the United Nations, which proposes *inter alia* consideration of negotiations on a Nuclear Weapons Convention or agreement on a framework of separate mutually reinforcing instruments backed by a strong system of verification." Gone was the statement in the earlier draft that the convention would "contribute" to the achievement of a world without nuclear weapons.

Also banished was the recommendation in a committee draft that the UN Secretary-General be invited to "convene an international conference in 2014 to consider ways and means to agree on a roadmap for the complete elimination of nuclear weapons within a specified timeframe, including by means of a universal, legal instrument."

Yet the reference to a Nuclear Weapons Convention that did survive is not toothless. For the first time in a Non-Proliferation Treaty document, the concept of a global ban, with all the work necessary to achieve it, is validated. In fact, grudging though it may be, the reference is given more heft by the statement preceding it: "The conference calls on all nuclear weapons states to undertake concrete disarmament efforts and affirms that all states need to make special efforts to establish the necessary framework to achieve and maintain a world without nuclear weapons." The nuclear weapons states doubtless interpreted the references to "convention" and "framework" as not binding and thus, in a gesture of goodwill for the sake of a successful ending, let them pass. Nonetheless, the concepts are now embedded and the advocates of a nuclear-weapons-free world have an agreed document they can build on.

Libran Cabactulan set out six principles for nuclear disarmament. These principles show the historic momentum that is building up for the abolition of nuclear weapons:

1. "The conference resolves to seek a safer world for all and to achieve the peace and security of a world without nuclear weapons, in accordance with the objectives of the [NPT]." This language is lifted from Obama's vision and unites governments in the final goal.

2. "The conference reaffirms the unequivocal undertaking of the nuclear weapons states to accomplish the total elimination of their nuclear arsenals leading to nuclear disarmament, to which all states parties are committed under Article VI." This language was first used at the 2000 Treaty review conference and was considered a breakthrough at

the time. During the Bush years in the first decade of the twenty-first century the US repudiated the statement, but at least the lost ground was recovered here.

3. "The conference reaffirms the continued validity of the practical steps agreed to in the Final Document of the 2000 NPT review conference." A decade ago, thirteen practical steps had been agreed on. These included the entry-into-force of the Comprehensive Test Ban Treaty, negotiations for a ban on the production of fissile materials, significant reductions in nuclear weapons of all types, and upholding the Anti-Ballistic Missile Treaty, designed to stop the development of missile defences. With the Bush administration trumpeting its rejection of most of these measures and the other nuclear powers falling silent under the US mantle, very little had happened.

4. "The conference reaffirms that significant steps by all the nuclear weapons states leading to nuclear disarmament should promote international stability, peace and security, and be based on the principle of increased and undiminished security for all." This language also appeared in the 2000 document, at the insistence of France and Russia, abetted by their nuclear colleagues. What it means is that the nuclear weapons states will take steps forward only if they are convinced that such action is in their security interests. And since they all claim that the reason they keep nuclear weapons is to enhance their own security, they can invoke this self-interest in rejecting any particular measure. To see this squirming away from commitment reappearing in the 2010 document is not a good omen, though it can be overcome by conclusive evidence that the maintenance of nuclear weapons by any state worsens its security.

5. "The conference expresses its deep concern at the catastrophic humanitarian consequences of any use of nuclear weapons, and reaffirms the

need for all states at all times to comply with applicable international law, including international humanitarian law." There is enormous potential in this principle, because it lays the groundwork for the outlawing of nuclear weapons. The earlier version of this principle, reaffirming "the need for all states to comply with international humanitarian law at all times," has been weakened by the nuclear weapons states' still claiming that the principle of self-defence can justify the use of nuclear weapons: thus, they argue, humanitarian law, which rules out nuclear weapons, can be trumped by other aspects of international law. But the stage is now set for new efforts to establish beyond any doubt that international humanitarian law rules out any conceivable use of a nuclear weapon.

6. "The conference affirms the vital importance of universality of the [Non-Proliferation Treaty] and calls on all states not party to the treaty to accede as non-nuclear weapons states…and to commit to achieving the complete elimination of all nuclear weapons…" This is a recurring principle more honoured in the breach. It is aimed particularly at India and Pakistan, which have made it abundantly clear they will not join the Non-Proliferation Treaty as long as it permits the nuclear weapons states to retain their arsenals. Nonetheless, the fact that the Treaty does comprise 190 states makes it nearly universal—an attribute not to be discounted.

NEITHER HEAVEN NOR HELL

In the Final Document's action steps, the nuclear weapons states were called upon to "promptly engage" in an overall reduction in the global stockpile of all types of nuclear weapons, to further diminish the role and significance of nuclear weapons in military doctrines, to take nuclear weapons off alert status, and to reduce the risk of their accidental use. These steps were put in the context of the continuing effort to "reduce and ultimately eliminate all types of nuclear weapons." Again, the word *ultimately* gives the nuclear weapons states an excuse for delay. Yet the thrust of the document is clearly to move the international community forward toward preventing the proliferation of nuclear weapons, achieving irreversible nuclear disarmament, and protecting the peaceful uses of nuclear energy.

The 2010 Final Document also identifies a number of steps states should take to improve their capabilities to detect, deter, and disrupt illicit trafficking in nuclear materials in an expanded effort to thwart the spread of technologies and materials for the production of nuclear weapons. Other steps facilitate the transfer of nuclear technology and materials to states that are in conformity with the treaty, so that the peaceful use of nuclear energy can be expanded.

The safeguards systems employed by the International Atomic Energy Agency are to be strengthened to make sure there is no diversion of nuclear materials intended for the development of peaceful energy to bomb-making capability. Since the world recognizes nuclear proliferation and terrorism as primary threats to international peace and security, one would think governments would give a priority to adequate funding for the very agency charged with safeguarding systems. Yet the reverse is true. The International Atomic Energy Agency, whose annual budget is $377 million (US), has been reduced to begging for more money to do its job. The Final Document contains a provision encouraging states to *donate* $100 million over the next five years to strengthen the agency. It is no wonder that civil-society activists question the good faith of the nuclear weapons states, which are all profligate in spending for nuclear modernization but stingy in financing safeguards systems. Bad faith has long been an unsavoury characteristic of the nuclear weapons states. Yet they have at last been brought to the recognition that the total elimination of nuclear weapons is the only guarantee against their use or threat of use. Logic should be a starting point for action.

On May 28, the final day of the conference, Cabactulan kept the delegates waiting for four hours before opening the proceedings, to permit Ambassador Ali Soltanieh of Iran to get instructions from his capital to join in the approval of the Final Document. The president knew that if he opened the document for discussion, Soltanieh, never bashful in proclaiming his anti-US views, would set off so much disputation that the Final Document would never be approved. Cabactulan enlisted the help of the leaders of Brazil and Turkey to phone Tehran authorities to accept the reality that the document was the best they could obtain and that it was in Iran's interests to accept it. Finally, Iran's approval was sent to Soltanieh. Cabactulan convened the meeting in the main General Assembly hall at 3:25 PM with the wry observation: "All eyes are on us." He immediately secured approval of some minor reports, then, turning to the Final Document and looking at the audience for barely a second, he declared it approved and banged his gavel. The delegates cheered.

The 2010 Non-Proliferation Treaty review conference advanced international thinking, even if it fell short on actions. For that reason, even Ambassador Abdelaziz of Egypt, who led off the round of final statements, said it was an important step forward toward the realization of the goals and objectives of the Treaty. "The outcome document we just approved represents, in our view, a basis for a deal we intend to vigorously build on in the next years." He then called for "prompt commencement of negotiations on a Nuclear Weapons Convention, as the route to realizing a world free from nuclear weapons by the year 2025." US Under Secretary of State Ellen Tauscher said the Final Document "reflects President Obama's vision." Russia's ambassador, Anatoly Antonov, hailed Cabactulan: "You have gone into the history of the NPT." China welcomed the "substantial results" and emphasized it supported an international treaty for the complete elimination of nuclear weapons. France said, "The outcome relaunched momentum." The UK: "A breakthrough after a decade of failure."

This praise from the nuclear weapons states signalled either of two possible reactions, but likely not both: they were happy the document did not commit them to any immediate distasteful action, such as comprehensive negotiations to actually banish all nuclear weapons, or they felt there was now an agreed basis for further work. Weighing both possibilities, Canada's ambassador, Marius Grinius, called the result "a modest product," but containing "seeds of hope." The best characterization of the conference came from the Mexican spokesperson: "While not bringing us to heaven, it does distance us from hell, the hell of nuclear war."

On the way out of the UN grounds, a couple of young women from the Women's International League for Peace and Freedom, which had monitored the entire conference, handed out Chinese fortune cookies to the delegates with a little note that said: "It's not good enough to believe in good fortune. Start a preparatory process on a Nuclear Weapons Convention—now."

3

Obama vs. Military-Industrial Complex

After the eight depressing years of the presidency of George W. Bush, I felt a new surge of hope when Barack Obama stood in Prague's baroque Hradcany Square on April 5, 2009, his forty-fourth day in office, and proclaimed "America's commitment to seek the peace and security of a world without nuclear weapons."

Refreshing as his statement was, Obama was by no means the first world leader to express the vision of a nuclear-weapons-free world. I was in the United Nations General Assembly on December 7, 1988, when Mikhail Gorbachev, then the President of the Soviet Union, gave a sweeping presentation of world reform, the breadth and depth of which stunned delegates. He renounced the use of force in foreign policy, especially of nuclear arms. The same year, Prime Minister Rajiv Gandhi of India, who was later assassinated, presented to the UN a detailed action plan for the phased elimination of nuclear weapons by 2010. Earlier, Prime Minister Olof Palme of Sweden, who was also later assassinated, had proposed the concept of "common security," stemming from an overriding conviction that, in the nuclear age, no nation can achieve security by itself.

Nor was Obama the first US president to express disdain for his own country's huge nuclear stockpiles. Ronald Reagan said, in his 1984 State of the Union speech, "A nuclear war can never be won, and must never be fought," and went on to discuss with Gorbachev, for a fleeting moment at a summit in Reykjavik, the total end of nuclear weapons. But Obama was certainly the first leader of his country to lift up the hopes of so many people around the world that the US government, hitherto one of the chief proponents of the supposed value of nuclear deterrence, might actually lead the way in dismantling the world's nuclear weapons architecture.

The Prague speech set out Obama's "concrete steps": a new strategic arms reduction treaty with Russia, US ratification of the test ban treaty, a verifiable ban on the production of fissile materials, a strengthening of the Non-Proliferation Treaty, an international nuclear fuel bank for civil nuclear co-operation, and a global summit on nuclear security. "The world must stand together to prevent the spread of [nuclear] weapons," he said. The speech was undoubtedly a prime reason he was surprisingly awarded, later that year, the Nobel Peace Prize. Of course, Obama's other early moves, such as winding down the Iraq war, ordering the close of the Guantánamo prison, and his respectful demeanour to the Muslim world in a speech in Cairo, would also have commended him to the Nobel committee. So hungry was humanity for a leader who would elevate political discourse after Bush's truculence that Obama was greeted with acclaim evoking strains of the "Hallelujah Chorus." One could almost feel the Nobel committee's desire to give him more strength to advance nuclear disarmament, to protect the environment, to help the poor, and to solidify human rights.

Obama, in short, empowered all those who felt beaten down by the surge of militarism following the terrorist attacks of September 11, 2001.

"Yes we can," his campaign slogan, was now applied to making the world a safer, more equitable home for humanity, a place where nuclear weapons, the horrible instruments of mass murder, would be consigned to the dustbins of history. So, in that sense, Obama's Nobel Peace Prize was not premature. In his Nobel acceptance speech, he called for "the continued expansion of our moral imagination" to equip us to strive for peace even in the midst of war. We do not have to live in an idealized world to still reach for those ideals that will make it a better place, he said. "The non-violence practiced by men like Gandhi and King may not have been practical or possible in every circumstance, but the love that they preached, their faith in human progress must always be the North Star that guides us on our journey." Human progress, not necessarily immediate accomplishment, is the Obama yardstick.

Obama's own books, *Dreams from My Father* and *The Audacity of Hope,* reveal him to be a highly intelligent, principled man who understands the culture of peace: respect for the dignity and human rights of all peoples and rejection of violence. But it is in David Remnick's absorbing biography, *The Bridge: The Life and Rise of Barack Obama,* that we discover his concentration on political pragmatism, which has been raised to an art form in his political home of Chicago. Obama knows how and, more importantly, when to compromise. "Half a loaf is better than none" may be a tired cliché, but it aptly expresses the Obama operating philosophy. If he has to give the nuclear labs piles of cash for their modernization programs in order to win the support of right-wing politicians for his arms reduction treaty with Russia, he will do it. If he has to promote incremental nuclear disarmament by opposing comprehensive negotiations for a global ban, that becomes the order of the day. If his outreach to Iran is accompanied by more UN sanctions against that country, so be it. Contradictions and trade-offs are a daily routine in politics, made even more imperative by what he called the "shellacking" he took in the 2010 midterm elections, in which the Democrats lost control of the House of Representatives and narrowly averted losing control of the Senate. What counts are poll numbers, always pointing to the shoals to be navigated on the way to the next election.

Obama is both a professor and a pol, a unique combination that enables him to point the way forward with great discernment and eloquence and then go into the trenches to wrestle his opponents. It is precisely because Obama is correctly perceived by those fearful of change as wanting to elevate his own country from the rot undermining its economic and social strength that he has so many enemies. At first, he sought to be a transformational leader; but to survive he has also had to become an artful dodger. He is not a purist in his philosophy. He is a practitioner of what he thinks is possible. And he has judged that the abolition of nuclear weapons in the foreseeable future is not possible. They are simply too deeply embedded in the American political and military structure.

At least Obama is honest in recognizing the constraints to his ambition. In his Prague speech, immediately after setting out his vision of a nuclear-weapons-free world, he said, "This goal will not be reached quickly—perhaps not in my lifetime." Nonetheless he set, by political standards, a quick pace. By that fall he had convened, for the first time in the UN's history, a summit of the Security Council to deal with nuclear weapons. A unanimous resolution pledged broad progress on long-stalled efforts to staunch the proliferation of nuclear weapons and to ensure reductions in existing weapons stockpiles, as well as control of fissile material. When I worked at the UN in the 1980s, I asked my Canadian colleagues why the Security Council, charged with maintaining the peace and security of the world, never dealt with the nuclear weapons issue. They looked at me quizzically as if I didn't understand that the permanent members of the Security Council are the very states that maintain nuclear weapons, so why would they mess with their advantage? Obama stirred up the high-level machinery.

A few months later, on April 14, 2010, Obama invited forty-six other world leaders to Washington to make the point that the nuclear risk is not confined to terrorism, but also lies in the growing number of nations refining huge amounts of nuclear fuels. Obama told his fellow leaders that the summit was only "one part of a broader, comprehensive agenda that the United States is pursuing—including reducing our nuclear arsenal and stopping the spread of nuclear weapons—an agenda that will bring us closer to our ultimate goal of a world without nuclear weapons." This summitry was augmented by a new Strategic Arms Reduction Treaty with Russia, requiring each nation to limit deployed strategic warheads to 1,550, down from 2,200, and deployed land-, air-, and sea-based launchers to 700, with updated measures to verify compliance.

"AS LONG AS NUCLEAR WEAPONS EXIST"

Periodically, the US administration produces a statement of its nuclear strategy called a Nuclear Posture Review. Bush's was considered regressive by disarmament activists because it reinforced nuclear capabilities and threatened nuclear responses in retaliation for conventional, chemical, or biological attacks. Obama's officials had to flesh out his vision of a nuclear-weapons-free world but not to create the impression that Obama was abandoning the US nuclear deterrent, which would have resulted in a backlash from the far right, dooming the Senate ratification of the reduction and test ban treaties. The Obama review that resulted was proof that politics lives by paradox. It pointed to a distant future without nuclear weapons, even as it committed the US to maintaining its nuclear deterrent far into the future. The review could not have been clearer regarding US intentions: "As long as nuclear weapons exist, the United States will maintain safe, secure, and effective nuclear forces, including deployed and stockpiled nuclear weapons, highly capable nuclear delivery systems and command and control capabilities, and the physical infrastructure and the expert personnel needed to sustain them. These nuclear forces will continue to play an essential role in deterring potential adversaries, reassuring allies and partners around the world, and promoting stability globally and in key regions." And yet, some balm was poured on these foreboding words in another part of the document: "It is in the U.S. interest and that of all other nations that the nearly 65-year record of nuclear non-use be extended forever."

In politics, the proof of intention is in the spending appropriations. Following the release of the Nuclear Posture Review, the White House announced that it intends to spend $180 billion over the next twenty years to build new nuclear weapons factories and to maintain and modify thousands of nuclear weapons and delivery systems. This is on top of existing budgets. The Administration plans to reduce the present nuclear weapons stockpile by creating a "more agile deterrent." Bluntly, the plan states, "A multi-year and steady investment in the modernization of the complex is an essential element of the [Nuclear Posture Review], allowing the United States to safely reduce the role of nuclear weapons." These plans make a mockery of Obama's call for a nuclear-weapons-free world. It was considered progress when the review specified that the US would not use nuclear weapons against states that do not possess nuclear weapons but are compliant with their obligations under the Non-Proliferation Treaty. The other side of this coin is that the US is prepared to use nuclear weapons against those who do possess them and against those states it deems are not in compliance with the Treaty (e.g., Iran and North Korea). The long-standing elements of the US deterrence doctrine remain in place, and the modernization of its nuclear arsenal continues.

In a nod to Obama's aspiration, the review mentioned that the US would initiate a national research and development program to support continued progress toward a world free of nuclear weapons, including expanded work on verification technologies; but compared to the many pages devoted to strengthening the existing nuclear systems, this was a pittance. Continued work on nuclear weapons was justified, the review concluded, because the conditions for abolition do not currently exist. "Among those are the resolution of regional disputes that can motivate rival states to acquire and maintain nuclear weapons, success in halting the proliferation of nuclear weapons, much greater transparency into the programs and capabilities of key countries of concern, verification methods and technologies capable of detecting violations of disarmament obligations, and enforcement measures strong and credible enough to deter such violations."

The Nuclear Posture Review, while bowing in Obama's direction, said, in effect, that his vision can't be implemented. Regional tensions, if not wars, do not permit the nuclear powers to shed their nuclear arsenals. But when has the world ever been free of regional tensions? Or when will it be in the future? In the convoluted logic that drove the nuclear arms race during the Cold War, safety from nuclear weapons still depends on their continued deployment. Obama, the politician, knows when he is up against an unmovable force.

HOWLS FROM THE FAR RIGHT

Even the expression of Obama's vision has been enough to unleash nuclear proponents, who claim that the president is undermining the security of the nation with his talk of nuclear zero. Former US Secretary of Defense James Schlesinger, who describes himself as a nuclear realist, says the US will continue to need a strong deterrent "more or less in perpetuity." The notion that we can abolish nuclear weapons "reflects on a combination of American utopianism and American parochialism…It's not based upon an understanding of reality." Two of his former senior officials, Douglas Feith and Abram Shulsky, claim that America's allies would lose confidence in a US that lost its determination to maintain a nuclear umbrella over its friends. "This will likely spur nuclear proliferation—not discourage it." Besides, they said, Obama's policy would make it harder for the government to maintain its nuclear infrastructure. "Why should a bright young scientist or engineer enter a dying field—especially when innovation is discouraged by support for a ban on weapons testing, and by renunciation of new weapons development?"

James Woolsey, former director of the Central Intelligence Agency, says: "From the standpoint of a Syria, Iran or North Korea, the fact that the United States is holding out the dream of zero nuclear weapons and forswearing modernization even as they progress toward their own weapons makes the US look more like [a] weak horse." The conservative columnist Charles Krauthammer lampooned Obama's Washington summit as "an exercise in misdirection," distracting attention from the looming threat of Iran. Some ridicule Obama, as if not having nuclear weapons would be an unbearable deprivation. As some headline writers put it, Obama is too much the nice guy in a world of rats.

Other critics, like Senator James M. Inhofe of Oklahoma, maintain that a nuclear-free world is a dangerous fantasy and the US dare not forego constantly updating its remaining stockpile of nuclear weapons to make them safer and more reliable. Even with Obama's announcements of increased funding for the nuclear weapons complex, the Republican leadership in the Senate held up ratification of the Strategic Arms Reduction Treaty for months and only relented when Obama spent a huge amount of political capital to make the case that national security demanded it. Clearly, were Obama to push hard for action now on global zero, he would set off a firestorm of protest in Congress, and the present charges against him that he is a weak dreamer would escalate to accusations of recklessness. The continuation of his presidency would be in doubt if the idea took hold in the public that he was jeopardizing the security of the American people. The conservative-oriented talk shows on radio and TV, fascinated with the simplistic anti-government fulminations of the reactionary Tea Party movement, have amply demonstrated their capability to magnify marginal protests to a roaring crescendo.

The essence of Obama's position—that nuclear weapons detract from, not add to, security—would be lost in the howls of the ignorant, who have long believed the propaganda of their own government that their safety depends on the US winning the nuclear arms race. It may be true that most Americans, when asked the question directly, favour a global treaty to ban all nuclear weapons, but this abstract approval is trumped by the fear driven into the populace by 9/11 and the need to fend off al-Qaeda with all the might the country possesses. The fact that nuclear weapons cannot stamp out terrorism, whose seeds are found in communities all over the world, including the US, does not carry much weight among those who see such weaponry as the pinnacle of strength. And in these dangerous times, they yell, strength, not weakness, is needed.

A STATE OF MILITARISM

Regardless of the aspirations (his critics would say "whims") of its president, the political structure of the US is built on the idea of military supremacy. In 1961, a few days before departing the White House, President Dwight D. Eisenhower, an acclaimed general in World War II, warned his countrymen about the growing power of what he coined "the military-industrial complex" to dominate the policy-making process. "In the councils of government, we must guard against the acquisition of unwarranted influence, whether sought or unsought, by the military-industrial complex. The potential for the disastrous rise of misplaced power exists and will persist." Eisenhower's reference, to the power of a rising class of military, business, and political leaders who thrived on promoting military buildups, was prescient.

The multi-billion-dollar infrastructure investments in US military machinery, not least nuclear, enrich the politically powerful laboratories, corporations, and lobbying firms that make up the military-industrial complex. Of the world's top ten defence contractors, whose sales total in the hundreds of billions of dollars annually, eight are American, including Lockheed Martin, Boeing, Northrop Grumman, Raytheon, General Dynamics, and Honeywell; the thousands of firms that sub-contract from them have all profited from the Iraq and Afghanistan wars. The Carnegie Endowment for International Peace estimated the cost of US nuclear weapons and weapons-related programs in 2008 exceeded $52 billion. US budgeted military spending in 2009 was nearly half the whole world's military expenditure of $1.5 trillion. When US spending on the Afghanistan and Iraq wars is added to the regular basic military budget of $664 billion, the full amount provides dramatic evidence of the cost of American military supremacy.

Since the rise of the modern state following the Westphalia agreements three and a half centuries ago, no country has been so powerful. The US maintains 737 military bases in 150 countries around the world. Apologists say this is to shore up America's friends. Critics maintain it is to preserve the present global order in which the vested interests of the US and its allies are continually protected and excessively rewarded. The exaltation of military values in the resolution of conflict, which leads to aggressive military preparedness and a dominant societal standing of the military class, has in the past half-century produced a state of militarism in the US. The culture of war is what drives US policy-making, and Obama, by himself, cannot seem to do much to counter that.

The Obama presidency has cut back on the Pentagon's braggadocio seeking of a US "full spectrum dominance" of air, land, sea, and space, but military spending drives forward, recession or not. Op-ed pages are replete with strategic analyses making the point that this is not the time to cut defence spending, when so many jobs are dependent on it. Local politicians in Great Falls, Montana, where 40 per cent of the economy depends on Malmstrom Air Force Base, resisted the Strategic Arms Reduction Treaty because it would close down underground missile silos in the area, resulting in fewer armed forces personnel to shop in area stores. The Pentagon has been diligent through the years in apportioning defence contracts throughout the country, resulting in local economies' becoming dependent on them. In turn, defence contractors and their allies fund political campaigns. Once elected, many politicians become defenders of defence-spending priorities, and not a few of them have, post-politics, joined defence firms as lobbyists. The corruption of policy-making in the US has become insidious.

Support for US allies is another argument advanced by the military-industrial complex, holding that cuts would unnerve friendly nations that depend on US overseas commitments. Defence cutbacks would be taken as evidence that American retreat has begun and that the country is in terminal decline. Obama is caught in a terrible dilemma. His own instincts may be to recognize that the US should be just a part of, not the dominant player in, the unfolding world, in which the rise of China and India, among other states, cannot be stopped, but he is surrounded by a political establishment whose very existence is predicated on America's superiority. Like it or not, Obama is forced to keep feeding the hungry monster of militarism.

All the other nuclear weapons states are just as guilty as the US in aggrandizing their military strength, and all of them have their own forms of industrialists and lobbyists who profit from the production and sale of arms of all kinds. The largest arms traders in the world are the permanent members of the Security Council. Russia maintains and is modernizing its triad of nuclear forces, and its official doctrine claims the right to use nuclear weapons in response both to a nuclear attack and to aggression against it with conventional weapons "that would put in danger the very existence of the state." The UK is modernizing its Trident submarine to give it a nuclear striking power for decades to come. France and China both point to their military programs as a source of their strength. Nor should many countries in the developing world, which spend far more on their military than on education and health, adopt a sanctimonious attitude. The world is steeped in militarism.

But it is the US—the strongest economic state, the cornerstone of democracy and champion of liberty, the self-proclaimed leader of the free world—that people look to for a political agenda that meets the demands for true human security in the twenty-first century. When a leader of such a country comes along with the personal credentials and oratorical skills to foster the full application of human rights, it is to be expected that his country's true mission will be put under the microscope.

"PROMPT GLOBAL STRIKE"

What are the United States' ambitions? The Nuclear Posture Review tried to offer some assurance of benignity: "Indeed, the United States wishes to stress that it would only consider the use of nuclear weapons in extreme circumstances to defend the vital interests of the United States or its allies and partners." But who is to define "vital interests?" And what, precisely, are "vital interests?" The preservation of the state? Or access to resources in an overcrowded, competitive world? The military-industrial complex, whose starting point in debate is not the delineation of a culture of peace, will put its spokespersons to work.

The review is not at all reassuring that a slight cutback in nuclear forces means the US is reducing its dependency on military strength. The document says flatly: "The United States will…develop non-nuclear prompt global strike capabilities. These capabilities may be particularly valuable for the defeat of time-urgent regional threats." "Prompt global strike" is the highly controversial war-fighting concept of tipping inter-continental ballistic missiles with powerful but non-nuclear warheads capable of obliterating targets anywhere in the world in less than an hour from launch. This is not as futuristic as it sounds, for specifications for its development are to be included in the 2011 Department of Defense budget. US unmanned drone aircraft striking the Taliban in Pakistan are already commonplace. War by computer with troops staying at home seems to be the wave of the future.

It can hardly be expected that Russia and China, and perhaps lesser states, will sit still watching the US achieve such capability for total world dominance. The blasé attitude of the US and Canadian media to the development of yet another tyrannizing weapon, which further destabilizes world politics, is truly alarming. Why would the other nuclear powers give up their nuclear weapons if the US perfects a super-strike weapon? The Nuclear Posture Review tries to reassure Russia and China that it would not use such a new weapon against them, because it is meant to extinguish regional conflicts. That misses the point: other major states are not going to cede total military superiority to the US.

The outlook is even more clouded when space weapons and missile defence systems are factored in. US plans and working budgets for the weaponization of space are an ongoing reality. Work is proceeding on the development of space-based kinetic-energy kill vehicles to destroy high-speed satellites in space. For this reason, Russia and China have tabled in the Conference on Disarmament in Geneva a draft treaty banning all weapons in space. Fortunately, Obama rejected the Bush space policy's unilateral stance, and has stated that Washington will co-operate in the development of space arms-control policies. The development of space weapons must be stopped as a prerequisite to banning nuclear weapons on earth. Similarly, the perfection of missile defences, an idea long cherished by the military-industrial complex, would only spur the development of new offensive nuclear systems that could penetrate them.

The abolition of nuclear weapons, then, is caught up in the refinement and development of weapons systems of all kinds. Nuclear weapons are, at the moment, the most egregious form of human assault. They are the worst instruments of destruction ever invented. Certainly, in the name of universal human rights, now being recognized as the bedrock of the civilization aspired to in the modern world, they must be abolished. Obama recognizes this, but he is not a solo performer, and two years into his presidency he is weaker than when he started. He is part of a system not friendly to visionaries. Nuclear weapons are part of the culture-of-war mentality, by which the military-industrial complex beneficiaries profit and are thus enabled to invest in even newer weapons systems. An enemy can always be found to "justify" the expenditure of more money in the pursuit of dominance, which is always presented in the name of security. The defenders of nuclear weapons like nothing better than to maintain that it would be only when the world is at peace, or close to it, that we could afford to dispense with the nuclear deterrent.

The elimination of nuclear weapons must be considered as an end in itself, which will also produce a world climate that will slow down, if not eliminate, advanced weaponry. To accept the cynical view that states, constantly striving for power, will never let nuclear weapons go, is to admit defeat in the struggle for peace and to accept that the planet will be torn apart by nuclear explosions. Obama, conflicted as he is, is not a cynic. Like President John F. Kennedy, he does not base his hopes on a sudden revolution in human nature, but rather on a gradual evolution in human institutions. He concluded his Nobel acceptance speech by saying: "We can acknowledge that oppression will always be with us, and still strive for justice. We can admit the intractability of deprivation, and still strive for dignity. We can understand there will be war, and still strive for peace."

Obama's progress by paradox approach is supported by some senior US statesmen, notably former secretaries of state George Schultz and Henry Kissinger, former secretary of defense William Perry, and Senator Sam Nunn, former chairman of the Senate Armed Services Committee, who, in a number of articles in the *Wall Street Journal,* have endorsed the value of a nuclear-weapons-free world. In official circles, nuclear disarmament achieved legitimization when it was blessed by such eminent figures. They coupled their approval, however, with a demand for significant investments in the nation's nuclear weapons production plants and its three national laboratories "to maintain a safe, secure and effective deterrent." They explained this two-pronged approach this way: "We must move in two parallel paths—one path which reduces nuclear dangers by maintaining our deterrence, and the other which reduces nuclear dangers through arms control and international programs to prevent proliferation." The non-nuclear states see these two approaches as mutually exclusive. Again, we see how the nuclear establishment in the US will countenance the vision of a nuclear-weapons-free world only if the US maintains its nuclear advantage until reductions reach zero. Other states will never agree to proceed in this fashion. The continuing US "double speak" is the trap for humanity that I have long feared. If Obama's credibility is to survive, the US must prove that it intends to actually achieve zero nuclear weapons.

CHANGING INSTITUTIONAL THINKING

Attacked from the right for even mentioning nuclear zero, Obama is also under criticism from the left for making nuclear disarmament impossible by funding nuclear weapons programs far into the future. Peace activists lambasted Obama's 10 per cent increase in 2010 in funding for the nuclear labs. Greg Mello, co-founder of the Los Alamos Study Group, which monitors nuclear disarmament issues, wrote in the *Bulletin of the Atomic Scientists* that the Obama budget is "a kind of pre-emptive surrender to nuclear hawks." Whether or not Obama has a disarmament "vision" is irrelevant, Mello claims. "What is important are the policy commitments embodied in the budget request..." Though praising Obama for his aspiration, he says that disarmament advocates are making the situation worse by silently acknowledging that no progress can be made without capitulating to the incessant demands by the nuclear establishment for more and more money.

Perhaps Obama is following the strategy of his illustrious predecessor Franklin D. Roosevelt who, in a storied account, told a visiting delegation pressuring him to adopt a policy that he agreed with them: "Now go out and put public pressure on me to be able to do it." In this respect, there is little public pressure on the president to abolish nuclear weapons. Disarmament advocates are valiantly trying to make their case, with logic and the momentum of history on their side, but they are virtually blacked out in the corporate-driven mainstream media.

Though Obama shows no signs of taking heroic measures to advance his country into a nuclear-weapons-free world, he is, in an institutional manner, trying to change national thinking; a necessary process if ever there is to be establishment support for starting negotiations on a global ban on nuclear weapons. His National Security Strategy, issued in 2010, bears the mark of an intellectual bringing the components of human security into a holistic policy. In a personal introduction, Obama contrasts the success of free nations, open markets, and social progress, all of which have accelerated globalization, with the intensified dangers we now face, ranging from international terrorism and the spread of deadly technologies to economic upheaval and climate change.

Obama called for a strategy of national renewal and global leadership for the common good. "The burdens of a young century cannot fall on America's shoulders alone—indeed, our adversaries would like to see America sap our strength by overextending our power." The US, he averred, will strengthen international standards through the rule of law. "The international order we seek is one that can resolve the challenges of our times—countering violent extremism and insurgency; stopping the spread of nuclear weapons and securing nuclear materials; combating a changing climate and sustaining global growth; helping countries feed themselves and care for their sick; resolving and healing conflict while also healing its wounds." Then came a statement revealing Obama at his best: "Our long term security will come not from our ability to instill fear in other peoples, but through our capacity to speak to their hopes."

While he says all this is America's mission, the agenda he sets out is a global one. That is unquestionably supportable by nuclear abolitionists, even as they lament his inability to lay out a timetable to get to his goal. Drawing on the wisdom of Chicago ward politics, Obama may be figuring that stealth is the best tactic to overcome political opposition. On the other hand, he may have no intention of fighting the military-industrial complex for the sake of his aspiration.

At a time when the US is trying to cope with an overextended foreign policy, which has led to two simultaneous wars and crippling debt, the idea of giving up its nuclear deterrent, if and when the idea is taken seriously, will be vigorously opposed by those who fear a further decline of America in the world structure. Already the US is in relative decline in terms of global gross domestic product, trade, and investment; and in social indices such as education, health, and urban infrastructure. The rise of competitor nations, such as China, India, and the new collective of the European Union, has already taken the shine off US stature as a superpower. Obama's fiercest political enemies, embodied in such manifestations as the Tea Party movement, cannot abide the inevitability that America will no longer be Number One in a globalized world, where the problems of human survival transcend national boundaries. They look to the sureness of US strength to overcome the anxieties and uncertainties of the future. They want America's might, not Obama's intellectualism.

Preparing the way for US leadership in getting to a world without nuclear weapons is, of course, essential. But politics demands deliverables. Good intentions are not enough. Having raised expectations, Obama will be judged not on whether a nuclear-weapons-free world was achieved in his lifetime, but on whether his presidency took measures, such as starting global negotiations in good faith, that truly advanced the goal. A legacy of sweet talk while feeding the voracious nuclear weapons complex will not impress future historians.

4

Canada: Nuclear Indifference

Murray Thomson, an eighty-eight-year-old peace campaigner born of Canadian missionary parents in Honan, China, is never without a smile and usually a wisecrack. A student at the University of Toronto when World War II began, he enlisted in the air force and became a pilot. He was still in training when the Hiroshima bomb exploded, an event, he says, "that changed my life completely." He later became a Quaker and developed a lifelong commitment to ridding the world of nuclear weapons. Early in his career he worked for Canadian University Service Overseas in Southeast Asia, and later he was instrumental in the founding of a number of Canadian peace organizations, including Project Ploughshares, the Group of 78, and Peace Fund Canada. As an Officer of the Order of Canada himself, he conceived the idea of soliciting fellow members of the Order, perhaps the most prestigious group of citizens in the country, to endorse an appeal to the Canadian government to support a Nuclear Weapons Convention. "Maybe," Thomson reasoned, "the government will listen to these important Canadians." Canada should support a Nuclear Weapons Convention, Thomson said, because "the vision of the elimination of all nuclear weapons, put forward by President Obama and many others today, requires the political will of governments for it to be achieved."

Thomson sought out John Polanyi, a University of Toronto scientist and 1986 Nobel Prize winner in chemistry, who shares Thomson's passion for peace, to help him. And he also approached me. Thomson began writing to members he knew, asking for more names and addresses. Soon he had a list of one hundred endorsers. Keep going, we urged. The number of signatures kept piling up, which showed, if anything, that public opinion about nuclear disarmament is very much alive in Canada.

In early 2010, with the list topping five hundred, we enlisted the help of Steve Staples, head of the Rideau Institute, a dynamic research and advocacy centre in Ottawa, to take the project public. We published the names in full-page ads in the *Hill Times* and the *Embassy*, newspapers that reach into all the Ottawa political offices. Celebrities galore were included: Margaret Atwood, Tommy Banks, Roméo Dallaire, Atom Egoyan, Graeme Gibson, Mel Hurtig, Norman Jewison, Peter Newman, Michael Ondaatje, Christopher Plummer, Fiona Reid, Veronica Tennant, John Turner, Jean Vanier. Several top-ranking businesspeople, who we thought would appeal to Prime Minister Harper, were listed: William Daniel, former president, Shell Oil; Adam Zimmerman, former president of Noranda and chair of the C. D. Howe Institute; Henry Jackman and Lincoln Alexander, former lieutenant-governors of Ontario. Also listed were Bruce Aikenhead, the architect who designed the Canadarm used in space; Ralph Barford, president of GSW Inc.; Timothy Brodhead, President of the J. W. McConnell Family Foundation; Purdy Crawford, corporate philanthropist; John Ellis, former vice-chairman, Bank of Montreal; Richard W. Ivey, CEO and chair, Ivest Corporation; and Pierre Jeanniot, general manager of IATA and former president of Air Canada. Definitely the "A" list of Canada.

We sought a meeting with the prime minister and were surprised to receive an appointment much earlier than we had anticipated. Stephen

Harper received us congenially in his Langevin Block office facing Parliament Hill at 3 PM on April 9, 2010, which was the Friday afternoon before Obama's Washington summit on nuclear security. We had originally sought an appointment a couple of weeks later, but his staff moved the date up, and we quickly surmised that our visit was to be part of his briefing for the imminent summit. Two aides were present and half a dozen thick files lay on his desk.

Thomson presented the prime minister with the Order of Canada signatures, and he seemed impressed with the scope of the list. I then handed him a three-page *aide-mémoire*, which concluded by suggesting, "It is a realizable and supportable goal for Canada to couple its existing work on the NPT with a commitment to support preparatory work on a convention or framework agreement providing a legal basis for the elimination of nuclear weapons. This could be backed up by Canada contributing its existing and praiseworthy skills in verification mechanisms, dispute resolution procedures, and enforcement provisions to the developing international dialogue." The prime minister said he was worried about Iran's pursuit of nuclear weapons and how proliferation could be stopped. Politely, he said he would take our suggestions under advisement. But when John Polanyi began to speak, Harper's attention became focused.

Polanyi, noting the prime minister's attendance at the forthcoming summit, said that Canada, carrying out its policy of opposing international commerce in highly enriched uranium, should return to the US some hundreds of kilograms of highly enriched uranium that it had accumulated over twenty years of irradiating it in the Chalk River reactor (and converting only 5 per cent into a medical isotope, molybdenum-99, which tracks and treats disease). Perhaps the return of this dangerous fuel could be announced at the Washington summit, he suggested. The prime minister made notes.

The following week in Washington, Harper announced that highly enriched uranium being held in Canada would be sent to the US to be converted into a form that could not be used for nuclear weapons.

"Canada recognizes that nuclear terrorism is an immediate threat to global security," Harper told reporters. "Terrorists could possibly use highly enriched uranium found in spent nuclear fuel to make bombs." Therefore, he said, the best defence is to store nuclear material in conditions of maximum security. Harper coupled this action with a new effort to help Mexico convert its weapons-grade fuel to a lower level. It appears the Order of Canada delegation had an impact on the prime minister, although not in the way we had originally intended.

It would be churlish not to acknowledge Harper's concern about the safety of nuclear fuels, but to limit action to this front and not address the principal question of substantively reducing nuclear dangers by getting rid of nuclear weapons and putting all nuclear fuels under strict international control is short-sighted. His action would have been more impressive if he had also demonstrated a concern to strengthen in a substantive way the Non-Proliferation Treaty and the International Atomic Energy Agency, the two instruments that do the heavy lifting in reducing nuclear dangers.

The Order of Canada project, calling for work to start now on a Nuclear Weapons Convention, supports a comprehensive way to eliminate nuclear dangers. Harper's briefing notes undoubtedly contained the foreign affairs department's favourite argument against a convention, that it is "premature," but at least he was sensitive enough not to use that argument in our meeting. The UN Secretary-General and a growing number of world leaders don't think it is premature. Now that the concept of the Nuclear Weapons Convention has been written into the Final Document of the 2010 Non-Proliferation Treaty review conference, it's time for Canada to take off its blinders and see the new direction of the nuclear disarmament debate.

Leading nuclear disarmament activists, such as Ernie Regehr, Jennifer Simons, Steve Staples, and Erika Simpson, are prodding Canada to move down this road. In November, 2009, Metta Spencer, editor of *Peace Magazine,* and an ardent campaigner against nuclear weapons, organized a two-day "Zero Nuclear Weapons" public forum in Toronto's City Hall, opened by Mayor David Miller. Mayor Akiba of Hiroshima appeared by videoconference and the celebrated New York writer Jonathan Schell appeared in person. The thrust of the discussions was to bring Canada back to its former place as a sure advocate for the elimination of nuclear weapons.

Two months later, Bev Delong, a Calgary lawyer who has, for several years, headed the Canadian Network to Abolish Nuclear Weapons, brought together sixty-five experts in Ottawa for a seminar entitled "Practical Steps to Zero Nuclear Weapons." Those attending included academics, civil-society representatives, and officials from the US and Canadian governments as well as from the UN and NATO. The key groups involved, the Canadian Pugwash Group, Physicians for Global Survival, Project Ploughshares, and the World Federalist Movement, go on doing responsible work. They publish critical analyses, generate mail to the prime minister, and their representatives visit MPs to bring them new information.

THE CANADIAN RECORD

By any criterion of political action—usually defined as action for enlightened self-interest—Canada ought to be in the forefront of supporting Obama's desire to rid the world of nuclear weapons as a step to a firm peace. The values that Obama espouses are the very values that Canada has traditionally tried to advance through its work at the United Nations. Canada, which used to think of itself as a bridge-builder, is in a position to create the international support Obama craves. Without the active support of key middle-power countries, which are playing an increasingly larger leadership role in the world, Obama will have a hard time convincing his domestic legislators to act.

This is not to suggest that Canada, whose thirty-four million people rank it only the thirty-sixth most populous nation in the world, is a major player in the new debate on the future of nuclear weapons. But a country that is the second largest in geographical size, with huge reserves of natural resources, high technology, and a skilled labour force, rated by the UN Human Development Index as the fifth best country in which to live, bears a considerable responsibility for the well-being of the planet.

Yet the Canadian government is practically silent on nuclear weapons, an issue Obama says is "fundamental...to the peace and security of the world" and on which he has, in political terms, stuck his neck out. As a co-occupant of North America with the US, as a strong ally and trading partner, as a nation that has followed the US lead in countless initiatives designed for mutual protection, Canada might have been expected to promote the Obama nuclear agenda.

To fully understand Canada's reticence, if not lassitude, we should look at Canada's past role in nuclear weapons issues. As a member of the Manhattan Project, which developed the atom bomb, Canada was the first country in the world to have the capacity to build a nuclear weapon and then renounce it. Ever since, Canadians have prided themselves on shunning the bomb—but that pride is somewhat misplaced. Starting in 1950, the US deployed Mark IV atomic bombs for use by its Strategic Air Command at Goose Bay. Later, Canada accepted Bomarc surface-to-air missiles from the US and, when the Diefenbaker Conservative government refused to equip them with nuclear warheads, the Liberals under Lester Pearson said they would and won the election of 1963. Soon after, the Canadian air force installed Genie air-launched missiles on fighter aircraft and also deployed anti-submarine nuclear depth bombs at Argentia Bay, Newfoundland. According to the estimates of John Clearwater, the leading researcher in this matter, some two hundred and fifty to four hundred and fifty nuclear weapons were deployed with Canadian forces in Canada and Europe.

It was Prime Minister Pierre Trudeau who ended Canada's direct involvement with nuclear weapons, although as a member of NATO Canada has always remained under the US nuclear umbrella. Even Trudeau's personal disdain for US testing of the cruise missile delivery system in Canada could not overcome US pressure, and permission was repeatedly given for such tests. In 1983, nearing the end of his term in office, Trudeau began visiting the nuclear weapons capitals with a plea to halt the nuclear arms race. "Trudeau's peace mission," as it was called, did not appear successful at first, but, as the decade developed, his efforts played a role in mitigating the antipathy of the Soviets and Americans to ending the arms race. In 1987, presidents Gorbachev and Reagan actually produced a treaty eliminating the intermediate-range nuclear missiles.

Canada's hands aren't entirely clean when it comes to nuclear energy, either. In 2009, the government signed a nuclear technology trade deal with India despite Non-Proliferation Treaty strictures prohibiting a transfer of nuclear technology to states with unprotected, that is, military, nuclear programs. The fact that India had violated regulations by using Canadian technology to set off a nuclear explosion in 1974 was all but forgotten. As the world's largest exporter of uranium, which, when highly enriched, becomes the fuel for nuclear weapons, Canada insists its uranium is used only peacefully. But uranium exports to the US are entered into a pool that supplies both military and civilian needs. Despite these inconsistencies, Canadian policy has always been to promote nuclear disarmament while benefiting from nuclear trade for peaceful purposes.

When Brian Mulroney came to power in 1984, one of his first speeches emphasized that the central issue confronting the modern world was the prevention of nuclear war and the need to inaugurate an era of assured peace for all. I found this a sign of hope for the future, and when Mulroney's foreign minister, Joe Clark, asked me to become Ambassador for Disarmament, I felt it was an opportunity. After twelve years in the House of Commons, I had decided not to run in the 1984 election in order to find a job where I could work full-time on peace and nuclear disarmament issues. The written mandate assigned three functions to me: to represent Canada at international meetings on disarmament and arms control, to be a special adviser to the government with direct access to the foreign minister, and to be the point of contact between the government and non-governmental organizations. When Clark, in his first speech at the UN, said that reversing the nuclear arms buildup "will be a constant, consistent, and dominant priority of Canadian foreign policy," I thought we were off to a good start.

The government had six main arms-control and disarmament policies covering a wide canvas: negotiated radical reductions in nuclear forces and the enhancement of strategic stability; the maintenance and strengthening of the nuclear non-proliferation regime; pursuit of a verifiable, multilateral Comprehensive Test Ban Treaty; negotiation of a global ban prohibiting the development, production, and stockpiling of chemical weapons; the prevention of an arms race in outer space; and confidence-building measures to facilitate the reduction of military forces in Europe and elsewhere.

The government buttressed this work by scientific advancement of verification techniques and formulating a set of verification principles accepted by the UN. Still, the overall effect of this work was vitiated by the raging US-Soviet nuclear arms race. Clark's good intentions could not withstand American pressure. Mulroney's major agenda was building goodwill with the US to get American co-operation on reducing acid rain and in accepting a free-trade agreement. Bringing up nuclear disarmament in Canada-US talks was considered an irritant. US Secretary of State George Schultz once bluntly reminded Mulroney and Clark that US security interests in the northern half of North America could not be interfered with by the Canadian government. The Canadian leaders recognized they were in no position to counter Schultz's obstinacy.

The US was firmly opposed to freezing the development of nuclear weapons. Thus the Canadian government voted against freeze resolutions at the UN and acceded to a US request to test an advanced cruise missile in Canadian airspace. Canada tried to find disarmament openings where it could, but generally the country was boxed in by strident US nuclear policies. US dominance put Canada in the contradictory position of working for nuclear disarmament while supporting the US's extension of the arms race.

Tensions over escalating armaments revitalized the peace movement in Canada during the 1980s. The Pugwash organization and Voice of Women were joined by growing numbers of physicians, scientists, and educators concerned by the threat to humanity posed by the spiralling arms race, which consumed scarce resources and held security hostage to ever-increasing expenditures. Their concerns found an outlet in the Consultative Group on Disarmament, a government-sponsored group of academics and activists, which I chaired. We met two or three times a year to discuss current peace and security issues. The government had also established the Canadian Institute for International Peace and Security to build public understanding of the issues related to international peace and security from a Canadian perspective. The institute became a focal point for peace groups demanding more government action in disarmament, which made it vulnerable to an emerging new strain of conservatism inimical to funding any group that criticized the government. It fell to the axe of budget cutting in the early 1990s. During these years, Canada was an outstanding leader within the United Nations Peacekeeping Forces, which won the 1988 Nobel Peace Prize. But Canada's interest in peacekeeping also withered with the spread of post–Cold War conflicts.

NATO'S CONTRADICTION

The latter 1990s were the high-water mark for productive interaction between civil society and the federal government, then led by Jean Chrétien. Working closely with non-governmental organizations, Foreign Minister Lloyd Axworthy called an international conference, which led to the Mine Ban Treaty. Axworthy also took a report from Project Ploughshares, based on consultations I led with civic leaders across the country, to Parliament, and mandated the foreign affairs committee to review Canada's policies on nuclear weapons. The parliamentary committee's chief recommendation was to have Canada lead the way in proposing that NATO review its Strategic Concept, whose central point was that nuclear weapons are "essential to preserve peace" and are "the supreme guarantee of the security of the Allies." NATO did conduct a review, starting in 1998.

By this time I had left the ambassador's post, had become a visiting professor at the University of Alberta, had assumed a new career as a senator, and was chairing the Middle Powers Initiative. When the NATO review started, I led a delegation to five key NATO states—Norway, Germany, Italy, the Netherlands, and Belgium—and also to NATO headquarters in Brussels. I brought a brief detailing how NATO's policies directly contradicted the commitment NATO states had made to the Non-Proliferation Treaty.

Government officials tried to keep a straight face as they averred, time and again, that there was no contradiction between calling nuclear weapons "essential" and making an "unequivocal undertaking" to eliminate them. It became clear, of course, that the real reason for their opposition was the adamant stand taken by NATO's three nuclear weapons states, the US, the UK, and France, to holding onto their arsenals. NATO officials saw the review as merely examining safety provisions with the possible advancement of confidence-building measures. As for examining the core doctrine of possession, this was out of the question. Canada's sincere efforts to get NATO to face up to its stultifying thinking were undermined when NATO bureaucrats began to refer to us as a "nuclear nag." The steam went out of Canada's efforts after Axworthy retired from politics in the fall of 2000. The NATO review was published, the status quo triumphed.

Rebuffed, Canada pulled back on nuclear disarmament initiatives and, all through the Bush years, kept a low profile on the subject. It was content to maintain what had long been heralded as Canada's "balanced" approach between support for the Non-Proliferation Treaty and UN work for nuclear disarmament on the one hand, and loyalty to NATO on the other. But the policy is not "balanced" at all. It is skewed by NATO's continued blockage of comprehensive nuclear disarmament.

The 2010 NATO summit repeated the decades-long mantra that "the supreme guarantee of the security of the Allies is provided by the strategic nuclear forces of the Alliance," which remain part of its "core" strategy. The latest edition of NATO's strategy put this iron fist in something of a velvet glove by stating, "We are resolved to seek a safer world for all and to create the conditions for a world without nuclear weapons in accordance with the goals of the Nuclear Non-Proliferation Treaty." As for actually backing the UN Secretary-General with at least a nod to global negotiations for a ban on nuclear weapons, not a word. NATO's duplicity amounts to a Catch-22 policy, because Russia and China will certainly not relinquish their nuclear weapons as long as the West's military alliance resists doing so. As for Canada, it continues to argue that the incremental steps to nuclear disarmament, such as a test ban and fissile material negotiations, must be completed before it can consider a Nuclear Weapons Convention. This very policy, "incrementalism," has been shown for the past forty years not to work because it does not attack the doctrine of nuclear deterrence, which various states claim to be the rationale for the maintenance of their arsenals, even if the arsenals are reduced. Thus, modernization of nuclear weapons continues while the major states ignore the one thing that will end nuclear weapons: a global ban. When the term "vicious circle" was coined, the originator must have had nuclear disarmament in mind.

In the past few years, Canada has consistently voted no, with most of its NATO partners, to any resolution at the UN Disarmament Committee calling for negotiations for a Nuclear Weapons Convention or for establishing a timetable for multilateral negotiations. Canada has raised its head above the surface only occasionally. In 2002 and 2003, Canada was the only NATO nation to vote at the UN for a modest nuclear disarmament resolution sponsored by the New Agenda Coalition, a group of middle-power states pressing the nuclear weapons states for more definitive progress. That was an act of courage, for Canada likes the "good company" of its alliance partners when it takes progressive steps. But the action was rewarded in 2004 when seven other NATO states joined Canada.

Since then, the subject has fallen off the table, with successive foreign ministers showing little interest, and officials quickly understanding that a posting to the disarmament bureau is not a career-advancing move. When Foreign Minister Lawrence Cannon gave the Canadian speech at the 2010 Non-Proliferation Treaty review conference, he made no substantive reference to disarmament, one of the treaty's three main pillars. In his first four years in office, Prime Minister Harper has virtually ignored the issue. Lawrence Martin's book, *Harperland*, a detailed account of Harper's first four years in office, contains not a single reference to nuclear weapons issues. Though not rejecting longstanding Canadian policy in support of the elimination of nuclear weapons, neither has Harper championed it at this moment of opportunity opened up by Obama's initiatives.

Canada's contribution to the Non-Proliferation Treaty review was confined to advocating annual conferences and to giving the treaty an institutional home, which are admirable objectives but do not address the core problems blocking nuclear disarmament. Harper renewed Canada's commitment of $1 billion to the G8 Global Partnership Program, which conducts such work as securing nuclear materials in Russia and redirecting weapons scientists to employment in civilian fields. While a necessary work to thwart terrorism, this is principally a non-proliferation measure, not nuclear disarmament. Harper did not use his opportunity in chairing both the G8 and G20 meetings, held in Canada in 2010, to put Obama's agenda of a nuclear-weapons-free world front and centre.

WHAT'S HAPPENING TO CANADA?

Under Harper, Canada's policies on nuclear disarmament have turned from ambivalence to indifference. In 2010, four senior statesmen, former Prime Ministers Chrétien and Clark, Axworthy, and former New Democratic Party leader Ed Broadbent, tried to break through this indifference in an unusual joint op-ed piece in the *Globe and Mail*, which sounded "a wake-up call to governments and people to deal urgently with the nuclear crisis…now before it is too late." But the prime minister's security concerns lie elsewhere. He has increased Canada's military presence in the Arctic. He has cast aside Canada's longstanding balanced position on the Middle East to champion Israel's controversial security moves. Canada's combat role in the Afghanistan war, which Harper inherited from his Liberal predecessor, has sapped increasing amounts of political attention and finances, as well as costing the lives of armed forces personnel.

It is in military spending that Harper shows his true priorities. The $21 billion defence budget for 2010 was a 10 per cent jump over the previous year and ranks Canada as the thirteenth-largest military spender in the world. It is the sixth-largest among the twenty-eight members of NATO. Yet Canada has sunk to sixteenth out of twenty-two donor countries in wealth devoted to official development assistance. Canadian military spending, now twenty times greater than the environment budget, is the country's highest priority. When the government announced it would spend $16 billion (including future servicing costs) for sixty-five new Joint Strike Fighter F-35s, most of the debate in Ottawa centred on the procurement process, not whether Canada needed more warplanes. The aerospace industry quickly mounted a campaign to defend the proposed purchase on the grounds it would produce high-quality jobs. Those who supported the Rideau Institute's argument that this was an irresponsible decision not based on Canada's security needs at a time the country was running a $54 billion deficit had a hard time getting public attention. The Canadian Centre for Policy Alternatives, an Ottawa-based think-tank, says the excessively high defence budget has come "at the cost of Canada's ability to contribute to UN peacekeeping operations and its ability to fund non-military contributions to global security and humanitarian action."

Harper inherited from Prime Minister Paul Martin a "3D" strategy— defence, development, and diplomacy—particularly for application in the Afghanistan war. Defence spending now completely dominates, and dwarfs the other two components. The aid budget is frozen and the government shows no signs of attempting to meet the international target of 0.7 per cent of gross domestic product to be devoted to official development assistance. The foreign affairs department is not only muzzled but significantly under-funded and, sadly, does not even try to practise the skillful multilateralism that, in former years, produced such Canadian giants on the international stage as John Humphrey, John Holmes, Hugh Keenleyside, Alan Beesley, George Ignatieff, and Saul Rae, all of whom I knew and greatly admired. The United Nations used to be a centrepiece of Canadian foreign policy. Not any more. Trade issues with the US and the Afghanistan war dominate the agenda.

On November 15, 2007, former Prime Minister Joe Clark spoke up against this narrow focus, trying to restore Canada's "long, proud, bipartisan history of international initiative." In a lecture to York University's McLaughlin College, he said, "We have become invisible on an international stage where Canada had been a consistent and constructive presence for more than half a century." But he was not heeded. Canadian diplomat Robert Fowler, who spent five months as an al-Qaeda hostage in western Africa in 2009 after being kidnapped while serving as the United Nations special envoy to Niger, criticized the major political parties for allowing special interests to dominate their foreign policy. "As the globe has become smaller and meaner, Canadian governments have turned inward and adopted me-first stances across the international agenda," he said. "Canada's reputation and proud international traditions have been diminished as a result." The *Embassy* newspaper excoriated Canadian foreign policy for becoming "more partisan than at anytime in recent memory." Louise Fréchette, a distinguished Canadian who was Deputy Secretary-General of the UN from 1998 to 2006, describes Canada's role at the UN today as "a shadow of its former self." "What's happening to Canada?" she wrote in *Canada Among Nations 2009–2010: As Others See Us*. "That's the question that greets Canadians visiting the United Nations nowadays…Our presence is only dimly felt." It is not only nuclear disarmament that has suffered in the new Canadian myopia. Though I was saddened, I was not surprised when Canada, for the first time in the sixty-five-year history of the United Nations, lost in the 2010 election for a seat on the Security Council.

CANADA'S SHIFT TO THE RIGHT

Obviously, there is not yet enough public outcry to pierce the ears of political Ottawa. When the Liberal Party unveiled its new foreign policy strategy, "Global Networks Strategy," in the spring of 2010, nuclear disarmament was scarcely mentioned. The New Democratic Party, the Green Party, and the Bloc Québécois all address nuclear disarmament in their policies, although with varying intensity. What is it that's making the central political establishment—Conservatives and Liberals—ignore an issue that not just advocates say is important, but that is one that the president of the US has put at the centre of the international political agenda?

Stephen Harper's ability to maintain power for four years, even with a minority government, is due not just to dexterous manipulation of the political agenda, such as closing down Parliament rather than face a vote of non-confidence he might lose, but to a shift taking place in mainstream politics. When I was elected to Parliament for the first time in 1972, running as a Progressive Conservative, the political posture of Canada was centre-left. It had been that way most of the time going back to Confederation. The Canadian attitude could be characterized as "reaching out." We reached out domestically in instituting health care for all and in

ensuring adequate funding for education. We reached out internationally by balancing our economic dependence on the US with multilateral
work through international agencies centring on the United Nations.
Immigration was recognized as adding to Canada's strength. Canada
shunned the paranoia of US "McCarthyism" and the self-absorption of
UK "Thatcherism." Even when Canada elected majority "conservative"
governments led by John Diefenbaker and Brian Mulroney, the notion of
social responsibility predominated.

The pendulum began to shift in the 1980s. Two competing views
clashed: the first supported the growing UN programs in sustainable
development and environmental protection and promoted moves to
restructure the world economy for the benefit of the poorest nations;
and the second espoused the neo-conservatism of the Reagan philosophy and opposed government intervention in the marketplace while
calling for massive military spending and foreign aid cuts. Conservatives
split, and bridging the widening gulf between Red Tories and the new
Reform element became unmanageable. The new Conservative Party
that emerged was far to the right of traditional conservatism.

The public mood shifted as the chaos of the post–Cold War years,
intersecting with the spread of globalization, rendered institutions,
domestic and international, less capable of maintaining economic and
social stability. When the terrorists struck on 9/11, what had been public
apprehension about the future turned to fear. There was a palpable
resurgence of militarism. Almost overnight, the protection of self, not
outreach to others, became the *leitmotif*. The Conservatives were in sync
with this new public mood, but they were not alone. The Liberal Party's
philosophy and demeanour moved to the right, and even the NDP, the
supposed bastion of socialism, all but abandoned its criticism of "corporate welfare bums," as a former leader once characterized the business
establishment. The political pendulum had swung to the right.

SOFT VS. HARD

In this environment, "security through strength," which had always been a conservative rallying cry, became a central theme: tougher crime laws, a stronger military, more money for protection. Working for nuclear disarmament lost its appeal. Since the public believed that the nuclear weapons problem had disappeared with the end of the Cold War, public pressure lessened almost to the point where the average MP never heard from constituents on the matter. For years, the media virtually ignored the issue—which, in any event, was seen as a "left-wing" issue. This did not mean there was any love for the bomb; rather there was indifference to its future in an agenda packed with a host of other security issues. The actual work of focusing on the complete elimination of nuclear weapons seemed to be an esoteric pursuit.

In latter years, the influence of the evangelical movement began to be felt in Ottawa, with a linkage between social conservatives and the religious right becoming a source of controversy in new battles about how much, if any, influence religion should have on politics. The evangelical movement is not noted for espousing any moral condemnation of nuclear weapons, which is an anomaly, considering its adherence to right-to-life positions. Evangelism and the rightward shift in Canadian politics seemed to blossom in the new climate. For its part, the military, which inordinately influences public policy, is not at all either sensitive or sympathetic to ridding the world of the one instrument that can bring about Armageddon.

The central political establishment sees nuclear disarmament as a "soft" issue, whereas the threats to world security require "hard" decisions. When the president of the United States presented his vision of a nuclear-weapons-free world, this would have been greeted warmly by earlier Canadian governments, freed at last to act on Canadian values for a safer, more equitable world. But when Obama presents his vision now, it doesn't resonate, and bureaucrats, accustomed to weathering the changing political climate, go on with their ordinary activities. Sooner or later, Obama will be gone. Why change?

In this period of treading water, enormous opportunities are being lost for Canada to play the role that used to be associated with its image. In the past, Canada stood out for its work in the principal human security issues in the world: development, nuclear disarmament, environmental protection, the advancement of human rights. Canada never tried to impose solutions, rather it worked creatively and publicly to bridge conflicting positions. The very exertion of ideas and influence seemed to strengthen the country as a middle power. At this new and significant moment, Canada needs to heed Obama's call and make the elimination of nuclear weapons a national priority. It needs to come out foursquare for a global legal ban on nuclear weapons, which could take the form of a Nuclear Weapons Convention or a framework agreement to encompass the various steps to elimination, such as a Comprehensive Test Ban Treaty and constant, phased reductions of nuclear weapons by all nuclear powers. It needs to shun its slavish adherence to the outmoded Cold War policies of NATO and to work actively with countries such as Norway, Germany, Belgium, Austria, and Switzerland that want all nuclear weapons legally banned. Canada needs to project once more onto the world stage the human security values that once lifted up this country.

Murray Thomson, for one, never gives up on his central idea that the Canadian government will move when the leadership in Ottawa senses a public shift in the thinking about nuclear weapons. His Order of Canada project has already had an outstanding success. In March 2010, he convinced Conservative Senator Hugh Segal to use the Order of Canada statement as the basis of a substantive motion Segal introduced in the Senate. At the heart of the motion was the phrase: "... encourage the Government of Canada to engage in negotiations for a Nuclear Weapons Convention as proposed by the United Nations Secretary-General." Three months later, the Senate unanimously passed the motion and sent it to the House of Commons for concurrence. Thomson, enlisting the aid of Conservative MP Scott Armstrong, then convinced the Government House Leader, John Baird, to put it forward under a procedure known as "unanimous consent." The House leaders of the other parties agreed, and on December 7 at 4:50 PM the motion, introduced by NDP MP Bill Siksay, sailed through the House in thirty seconds. It was the first time in the history of the Canadian Parliament that both chambers had united on a move calling for negotiations for a legal ban on nuclear weapons. Although the motion is not binding on the government, it will be hard for the cabinet to dismiss the expressed view of both the House of Commons and the Senate, backed by 535 members of the Order of Canada, a group of considerable influence. Don't tell Thomson the country won't get behind a Nuclear Weapons Convention.

PART TWO

THE VALUES DEBATE

5

Nuclear Weapons or Human Rights?

Listening to former US President Jimmy Carter describe his personal agony at possibly having to order a nuclear weapons strike was the most poignant moment I ever experienced in a long career dealing with nuclear disarmament issues. A junior naval officer for a number of years, Carter entered politics in his native Georgia, rising to governor, then to president of the US in 1976. The American hostage crisis in Iran in 1979 severely weakened him and, the following year, he lost the presidency to Ronald Reagan. He went on to found the Carter Center as a place to advance human rights and alleviate unnecessary human suffering. The centre has become famous for its work in monitoring elections and mediating civil conflicts. In 2002, Carter was awarded the Nobel Peace Prize.

A few months before the 2000 Nuclear Non-Proliferation Treaty review conference, Carter invited the Middle Powers Initiative to convene a meeting of some twenty key states and senior US officials to find common ground for progress on the nuclear agenda. His criticism of the major nuclear powers for not honouring the agreements they had made was withering. "If you look at the political debates going on between the Republicans and Democrats, not one word is mentioned of non-proliferation or nuclear agreements or some of the policies our own country has adopted or failed to adopt." In 2005, he invited the Middle Powers Initiative back and again he spoke. Our third visit was in January, 2010. He sat beside me at the long conference table, looking fresh and vibrant even at eighty-five. "Mr. President," I said when I spoke, "Here we are again. We're not getting older, we're getting better!"

Carter began his remarks by making it clear that the Obama moment would become productive for nuclear disarmament only if civil society is "aggressive, persistent, and demanding" of all governments. The overall vulnerability to nuclear attack had hardly improved over the years. "I was fully committed to respond if I was informed of a threat of nuclear weapons use against my country. With our land-based silo missiles, I know I had about a twenty-six-minute interval from the time of launch until they struck Washington, DC, or New York, and I was prepared to respond and destroy Russia as much as I could as well. We could have wiped out every city in Russia with a population of one hundred thousand or more with nuclear warheads from one of our submarines..."

In the question-and-answer period, David Krieger, president of the Nuclear Age Peace Foundation, returned to this sobering matter. How could the president reconcile his moral, religious, and spiritual values with nuclear retaliation, knowing the horrible consequences of such weapons? he asked. There was not a sound as we waited for the reply. "The most difficult question I've ever had to face as a human being is what to do if a nuclear threat materialized when we were in the midst of the Cold War. I prayed constantly that I would not be faced with this decision." Although he didn't see the rationality of nuclear weapons, "I couldn't sit acquiescently and let the Soviet Union destroy my country without a response when we had the capability to do so."

He said he bent over backwards to understand the paranoid concerns of the Soviet leaders, trying to figure out what might trigger a nuclear war and what could be done to avoid one. Then came the riveting words: "I can't say in good conscience now that my decision to respond would have been the correct one. It would have cost millions of American lives if we were subject to attack and it would have cost millions of Russian lives if we attacked. I cannot answer your question adequately. It is incompatible with my basic Christian beliefs to do that. What Jesus Christ would have done, I don't know. When I took the oath of office of president, before God, I took the oath to defend my country. I felt that was the way I could prevent further destruction of my country. The fact that the Russians believed I would respond was the essence of mutual deterrence. If I made any sort of public insinuation that the Russians could attack us with nuclear weapons without being the recipient of a response—that would have been unacceptable, unimaginable for me to do."

In those few words, President Carter revealed the impossibility of reconciling the use of nuclear weapons with the demands of conscience. He knew his answer was unsatisfactory. His humanity told him not to use nuclear weapons; his office, as he interpreted it, might require him to do so to protect his country. It is an impossible position to put a conscientious leader in. Yet that is what the policy of nuclear deterrence, the threat to use nuclear weapons against an adversary in the event of a perceived attack, does. It strips the humanity not only from the leader but from the society that deludes itself that this is a rational policy. It leads to a corollary: mutually assured destruction (sometimes known as MAD), which is that each opponent knows it has the power to inflict unacceptable damage on the other in the event of an attack. For decades, the public has allowed itself to be bamboozled into thinking that these are sane policies.

WHAT A NUCLEAR WEAPON DOES

It takes a reminder every so often of exactly what a nuclear weapon does, to restore a human rather than mechanistic response to instruments of mass murder—which is what nuclear weapons should be called. Such a reminder was offered by Jakob Kellenberger, president of the International Committee of the Red Cross, on the eve of the 2010 Non-Proliferation Treaty review conference. Kellenberger, a former Swiss diplomat, heads a body that prides itself on being an impartial and independent organization with the exclusively humanitarian mission of protecting the lives and dignity of victims of armed conflict and of providing them assistance. The Red Cross was one of the pioneers of the Geneva Conventions, dating back to 1864 and updated through the years to set the standards in international law for humanitarian treatment of the victims of war. Less than a month after the Hiroshima attack, the Red Cross called for nuclear weapons to be banned. It has consistently argued that the mere threat to use such indiscriminate weapons repudiates humanitarian law, which centres on the protection of the innocent.

Kellenberger began by quoting the testimony of Dr. Marcel Junod, a Red Cross doctor who was the first foreign doctor in Hiroshima to assess the effects of the atomic bombing. "We witnessed a sight totally unlike anything we had ever seen before. The centre of the city was a sort of white patch, flattened and smooth like the palm of a hand. Nothing remained…Thousands of human beings in the streets and gardens in the town centre, struck by a wave of intense heat, died like flies. Others lay writhing like worms, atrociously burned…Every living thing was petrified in an attitude of acute pain." There was virtually no medical help available because most of the doctors, nurses, and pharmacists had been killed. The transportation, food distribution, and water systems were all destroyed. Survivors of the attack faced life-threatening dehydration, diarrhea, and gastrointestinal tract infections. The radiation generated by the blast produced cancers and genetic damage in survivors and future generations.

Kellenberger said, "Nuclear weapons are unique in their destructive power, in the unspeakable human suffering they cause, in the impossibility of controlling their effects in space and time, in the risks of escalation they create, and in the threat they pose to the environment, to future generations, and indeed to the survival of humanity." Since the suffering from nuclear warfare is more than any civilization can bear, "the rights of states must yield to the interests of humanity." The nuclear weapons debate, he said, "must ultimately be about human beings, about the fundamental rules of international humanitarian law, and about the collective future of humanity." This is precisely the approach long taken by International Physicians for the Prevention of Nuclear War, 1985 Nobel Peace Prize winner, in warning that a nuclear war would produce an unlivable world. IPPNW brought out a new study in time for the 2010 Non-Proliferation Treaty meeting, providing an "unvarnished understanding" of the prospects of nuclear famine, nuclear winter, and nuclear mass murder unless nuclear weapons are abolished.

The term "Nuclear Famine" refers to the starvation that would ensue after a nuclear explosion. Even a limited nuclear war in one region, for example, South Asia, would result in millions of deaths, firestorms with soot rising into the upper troposphere, cooling temperatures, and a significant decline in food production. Prices for basic foods would shoot up, making food inaccessible to poor people in much of the world. Famine on this scale would also lead to major epidemics of infectious diseases, and would create immense potential for mass migrations, civil conflict, and war.

"Nuclear Ozone Hole" describes another consequence of nuclear war. Soot from burning cities in a nuclear war would severely damage the Earth's protective ozone layer. Large losses in stratospheric ozone would permit more ultraviolet radiation to reach us, with severe consequences such as skin cancers, crop damage, and destruction of marine phytoplankton. The effects would persist for years.

Two decades ago, the renowned scientist Carl Sagan coined the term "Nuclear Winter" to describe the global ecological destruction that would result from a massive nuclear exchange between the US and the former Soviet Union. A nuclear war would be followed by rapid drops in temperature and precipitation, blocked sunlight, and the collapse of agricultural production for at least a year, leading to death by starvation for huge numbers of the world's population. New studies have found that nuclear winter would be even longer than previously thought, with the decrease in food production lasting for many years.

In the decades following the atomic bombings of Hiroshima and Nagasaki, the medical effects of nuclear weapons have been documented in painstaking detail. In addition to killing virtually everyone within one kilometre, the blast would turn bricks, lumber, furniture, and cars into deadly missiles. The injured would suffer massive burns, ruptured organs, and fractured skulls, and would be blinded and deafened. The radiation exposure would produce diseases, in both the present and future generations.

NO LAW BANNING NUCLEAR WEAPONS

How can nations that pride themselves on their civilization descend to the barbarism of nuclear weapons? A short answer is that our governmental process has not yet matured to the point of protecting people against omnicide, the death of all. An individual murder on a street corner, yes. But fireball death from the skies indiscriminately killing thousands, no. It is hard to believe that in the twenty-first century, when successful globalization depends on the uninterrupted interplay of commerce and politics, there is no law prohibiting nuclear weapons that would destroy the very fabric of modern life.

No legal expert has spoken out more eloquently against nuclear weapons than Judge Christopher Weeramantry, the acclaimed former vice-president of the International Court of Justice, the highest legal authority in the world. In 1996, in a landmark decision, the court rendered an Advisory Opinion that the threat or use of nuclear weapons would generally contravene the rules of international law applicable in armed conflict. Judge Weeramantry said at the time, "My considered opinion is that the use or threat of use of nuclear weapons is illegal *in any circumstances whatsoever*" (emphasis his).

Born in Sri Lanka in 1926, Christopher Weeramantry obtained his doctorate in laws from London University; moved to Australia for a long teaching career that at one stage included a visiting professorship at McGill University's Institute of Sustainable Development; and, in 1990, was elected to fill the Asian seat on the International Court of Justice (often called the World Court). He retired from the Court in 2000 and opened the Weeramantry International Centre for Peace Education and Research in Sri Lanka. In 2006, he was awarded the UNESCO Prize for Peace Education and, the following year, the Right Livelihood Award. His *Nuclear Weapons and Scientific Responsibility* is the major text on the legal responsibilities of nuclear scientists.

I have heard him lecture several times. Short in stature and soft of voice, he exudes what one of his colleagues calls "a sweetness of soul." But his criticism of those who countenance nuclear weapons is sharp: "Any nation which does not take the steps to fulfill its obligation to rid the world of nuclear weapons cannot claim any longer to be concerned with human welfare and the human future."

Weeramantry's basic position is that the nuclear bomb stands categorically condemned by a dozen basic principles of international law. The bomb "represents the very negation of the humanitarian concerns which underlie the structure of humanitarian law." This is the "living law" and represents the high-water mark of legal achievement in the difficult task of imposing restraint on the brutalities of unbridled war. "Retaining a nuclear weapon arsenal is a flagrant violation of these rules and a betrayal of the duties owed by powerful states to the entire world community." He gives a homely example of the application of law: "There cannot be one law for the nuclear powers and another law for the non-nuclear powers…No policeman can enforce a law which the policeman himself openly violates."

Why does Weeramantry's view not prevail in legal circles? The answer lies in the lack of proper enforcement of world laws, and in a division of opinion within the World Court that weakened its ruling.

Although there are global treaties banning chemical weapons and biological weapons, there has never been a global law prohibiting nuclear weapons. The best that the Non-Proliferation Treaty can do is to call for the pursuit of negotiations for elimination. In the early 1990s, a movement started to request the World Court to rule on the legality of nuclear weapons. It is a weakness of the Court that its rulings are not enforceable unless disputant parties agree. Nevertheless, in 1994 a team of civil-society experts succeeded in having the UN General Assembly adopt a resolution requesting the Court's opinion. The case turned out to be the largest in the Court's history.

Of the forty-three governments submitting written opinions, two-thirds held that nuclear weapons were illegal under international law. But the US, the Russian Federation, the UK, and France all testified that the Court did not have jurisdiction to render an opinion and, in any event, the possession of nuclear weapons for deterrence or for self-defence is legal. These states also contrived to keep the International Criminal Court, when it was established in 1998, from explicitly specifying that the use of nuclear weapons would constitute an international crime. Crimes against humanity are defined as widespread or systematic attacks directed against a civilian population, carried out to further a state's policy; and war crimes include attacks on civilians or having a disproportionate effect on civilians and the environment. Nuclear weapons easily fall into these statutory definitions, and advocates hope that further work will result in nuclear warfare's being codified as a specific international crime.

The nuclear states certainly did not agree when the World Court ruled, in 1996, that the threat or use of nuclear weapons would generally contravene the rules of international law applicable in armed conflict. The Court said, "The destructive power of nuclear weapons cannot be contained in either space or time." In other words, the rule of discrimination, prohibiting the use of weapons that cannot discriminate between military targets and non-combatant persons or objects, would be violated. So would the rule of proportionality, which prohibits the use of a weapon whose potential collateral effects on civilians would be disproportionate to the military advantage. Nor may states use more force than necessary to achieve a military objective.

A STINGING INDICTMENT

Although the Court held that the use of nuclear weapons seems "scarcely reconcilable" with respect for humanitarian law, it could not conclude with certainty that their use would contravene international law in every circumstance. The Court recognized the reality of the strategy of nuclear deterrence "to which an appreciable section of the international community has adhered for many years." Accordingly, in view of the present state of international law viewed as a whole, the Court "could not reach a definitive conclusion as to the legality or illegality of the use of nuclear weapons by a state in an extreme circumstance of self-defence, in which its very survival would be at stake."

Because international stability suffers from these divergent views, nations are obliged, the Court said, "to achieve a precise result—nuclear disarmament in all its aspects." Calling attention to Article VI of the Non-Proliferation Treaty, the Court ruled unanimously: "There exists an obligation to pursue in good faith and bring to a conclusion negotiations leading to nuclear disarmament in all its aspects under strict and effective international control."

The president of the Court, Judge Mohammed Bedjaoui of Algeria, anticipated that the Court's inability to give an unqualified condemnation of nuclear weapons would be perceived by the nuclear states as a sort of acceptance, if not a blessing, for their nuclear arsenals—which is exactly what happened, in spite of his warning that the Court's inability to go any further should not "in any way be interpreted as leaving the way open to the recognition of the lawfulness of the threat or use of nuclear weapons."

He then gave a stinging indictment of nuclear weapons: "The very nature of this blind weapon…has a destabilizing effect on humanitarian law, which regulates discernment in the type of weapon used. Nuclear weapons, the ultimate evil, destabilize humanitarian law, which is the law of the lesser evil. The existence of nuclear weapons is therefore a challenge to the very existence of humanitarian law, not to mention their long-term effects of damage to the human environment…"

When I read that passage at the time, the words "the ultimate evil" stuck in my mind, and I wrote to Judge Bedjaoui for permission to quote him and to ask if he would provide the foreword to a book I was then writing, which was eventually entitled *The Ultimate Evil*. He graciously agreed, and again made the point that humanitarian law prohibits the use of weapons that have indiscriminate effects and are liable to cause unnecessary suffering. As for a state's claiming it had a right to use nuclear weapons in self-defence, he wrote, "It would be quite foolhardy to set the survival of a state above all other considerations, in particular the survival of mankind itself." Then he noted: "The medical world teaches us that madness is not a contagious disease. But international policy obeys different rules. The proliferation of nuclear firepower is by no means under control, despite the existence of the Non-Proliferation Treaty. So fear and madness may still link arms to engage in a final dance of death."

Judge Weeramantry was in a conflicted position as a result of the convoluted system of voting used by the Court. He agreed, of course, with the basic finding that the use of nuclear weapons would generally contravene all aspects of humanitarian law, but he could not agree with the indecision on the legality of their use in "an extreme circumstance of self-defence." In other words, he couldn't live with the loophole the Court had provided the nuclear powers, who, of course, seized on this narrow point of indecision and claimed that their conduct was legal. Weeramantry then wrote a long dissenting opinion, which stands today as the most comprehensive and compelling legal condemnation of any use of nuclear weapons. In short, he argued, "Nuclear weapons contradict the fundamental principle of the dignity and worth of the human person on which all law depends." And the weapons "endanger the human environment in a manner which threatens the entirety of life on the planet."

In his post-court role, Judge Weeramantry began leading a group of lawyers determined to find a way to get the World Court to take up the issue again and rule whether the nuclear weapons states are in "good faith" fulfilling their obligation to negotiate nuclear disarmament while modernizing their nuclear arsenals. "More than a decade has passed since the Court so categorically formulated this obligation, and yet we see a continued readiness to develop nuclear weapons and maintain nuclear arsenals," Weeramantry said.

The words from such jurists as Mohammed Bedjaoui and Christopher Weeramantry extend beyond the strictures of law to the primal notions of life and death. The subject of nuclear weapons must be dealt with from a legal basis, of course, and that is why the movement to build a Nuclear Weapons Convention, which would be a global legal ban on all nuclear weapons, is so important. But even deeper than this, nuclear weapons, with their massive, almost unlimited, destructive power, violate the process of life itself. Judge Bedjaoui was right: nuclear weapons are not just an instrument to prevent evil; they are evil themselves. They mock humanitarian law, displacing it with raw power. They are inimical to everything that life reflects: beauty, goodness, wholeness, hope. They violate the essence of humanity.

The legal, moral, military, and political objections to nuclear weapons all stand on the basis of our humanity. The most practical way to express that humanity is through building a culture of peace.

DEVELOPING THE HUMAN RIGHT TO PEACE

Two decades ago, the United Nations Educational, Scientific and Cultural Organization (UNESCO) began to formulate what it called a "culture of peace," which it defined as an approach to life that seeks to transform the cultural tendencies toward war and violence into a culture where dialogue, respect, and fairness govern human relations. The organization published a set of values making up a culture of peace: respect for life and the dignity and human rights of individuals; rejection of violence; recognition of equal rights for men and women; support for the principles of democracy, freedom, justice, solidarity, tolerance, and the acceptance of differences; communication and understanding between nations and countries and between ethnic, religious, cultural, and social groups.

The culture of peace is, at its core, an ethical approach to life. It recognizes that the world is experiencing a fundamental crisis. Though this crisis is often expressed in economic, ecological, or political terms, it is essentially a crisis of the human spirit. It is a crisis of humanity, which, in the journey through time, has reached the point where we are capable of destroying all life on earth just at the moment when the idea of inherent human rights is beginning to take hold.

A team of Nobel Peace Prize laureates drafted a set of guidelines for action, centring on respect for the life and dignity of every human being; the rejection of physical, sexual, psychological, and economic violence; a spirit of sharing to put an end to political and economic oppression; and dialogue to resolve fanaticism, defamation, and the rejection of others. The UN General Assembly designated 2001–2010 the International Decade for a Culture of Peace and Non-violence for the Children of the World. Programs on environmental protection, the advancement of human rights, sustainable development, democracy, and nuclear disarmament were started by more than a thousand organizations in a hundred countries.

Then the terrorists of 9/11 struck, and the resurgence of militarism followed. In the new environment of fear, the culture of peace has had a hard time being heard. One of its foremost champions is Ambassador Anwarul K. Chowdhury, a former United Nations Under-Secretary-General from Bangladesh, who steered the program through the UN.

He received the UNESCO Gandhi Gold Medal for Culture of Peace. An unusual diplomat, he has maintained a relentless concern for the poor and vulnerable. In his report at the conclusion of the decade, Chowdhury said the culture of peace should be seen as the essence of a new global civilization. "The flourishing of a culture of peace will generate the mindset in us that is a prerequisite for the transition from force to reason, from conflict and violence to dialogue and peace."

A NEW DEBATE ON NUCLEAR WEAPONS

As the ideas of a culture of peace slowly take hold in society, a future, more informed public debate may force the political system to face its responsibility to avoid war. The debate inevitably will centre on the deeply controversial question of the future of nuclear weapons. The World Court's landmark ruling has already framed the discussion by setting in motion an examination of the human rights of those affected by nuclear blasts, not just the supposed rights of the states to conduct nuclear warfare. The 1995 and 2000 Non-Proliferation Treaty review conferences moved the humanitarian case for elimination forward. It is painstaking progress, as the 2010 Treaty review conference showed, but at last the protest in the name of humanity has achieved diplomatic legitimacy, however feeble. A further examination of how the inhumanity of nuclear weapons scars the whole human landscape now needs to enter public debate.

For a long time, the nuclear disarmament debate consisted of abolitionists arguing with nuclear defenders over the pace of reductions. Technocrats always won those arguments, because they premised their case for nuclear deterrence as having value. It had the value, they said, of preventing nuclear war. That was the reason to maintain arsenals, so serious nuclear disarmament had to be put off to another day. But a new day arrived with the 2010 Non-Proliferation Treaty consensus Final Document's expressing its deep concern at the catastrophic consequences of the use of nuclear weapons and stipulating "the need for all states at all times to comply with applicable international law, including international humanitarian law." With the international community now focused as never before on the inherent inhumanity of nuclear weapons, the legal justification for their retention is crumbling.

Yet the defenders of nuclear weapons won't let go. Logic and the right of humanity not to be blown out of existence do not move them. That is why President Carter made his plea to nuclear weapons abolitionists to be "aggressive, persistent, and demanding" in claiming our full human rights. In his dogged pursuit of democracy and the full implementation of human rights around the world, Carter is a role model for me. He likes to say: "For this generation, ours, life is nuclear survival, liberty is human rights, the pursuit of happiness is a planet whose resources are devoted to the physical and spiritual nourishment of its inhabitants." That is the holistic thinking required to deal with intransigent politicians, who still don't understand that globalization has made the world a single entity.

President Carter sees the struggle for abolition in the context of the wide agenda of human security problems. The nuclear weapons problem does not exist in a vacuum. It is competing for attention in a field of challenges: chronic armed conflict, economic disruption, burgeoning pollution and climate change, energy deficits, unrelenting hunger, and grossly inadequate health and education services. All these subjects constantly demand public attention. Nuclear disarmament should not be viewed as just one more issue. This problem has the potential to destroy the structure of the world on which all the other problems depend for their solution.

The greatest threat to the environment by far would be a nuclear war. The poor of the world will be incalculably worse off in the aftermath of a nuclear attack in any region. The parade of steady human rights advances will be swept aside by the imposition of a drastic curtailment of civil rights following a nuclear blast. The campaigners for the other elements of the human security agenda should promote nuclear

disarmament as a priority in meeting their own goals. And abolitionists must work with others in the creation of a new, post-nuclear
security architecture.

Presidents Carter and Obama are two examples of thinking politicians.
The political system is by no means devoid of leaders who understand
that the architecture of nuclear weapons needs to be dismantled. Now
they need to be joined by a new generation of human rights activists
who will build a new architecture of security.

6

What's Another Billion Dollars?

At first glance, Bangladesh and nuclear weapons seem to have little in common. The image of Bangladesh, a low-lying land of 160 million people squeezed between India and Myanmar on the Bay of Bengal, is one of endemic poverty. Nuclear weapons are the instruments by which the great powers flex their muscles and dominate the world political system. What interest would Bangladesh have in the nuclear disarmament debate?

A month before the 2010 Non-Proliferation Treaty Review Conference opened, the Bangladeshi parliament unanimously adopted a resolution giving full support to UN Secretary-General Ban Ki-moon's nuclear disarmament plan and proposed Nuclear Weapons Convention. The resolution urged that the annual $100 billion spent globally on nuclear weapons be diverted to climate change adaptation programs and human development goals. The foreign minister of Bangladesh, Dr. Dipu Moni, in assuming the presidency of the sixty-one-nation Conference on Disarmament in Geneva a few months previously, made a strong plea to that moribund body to start action resulting in lower military expenditures, especially now, when the global financial and economic crisis is rolling back development gains in the poorest nations. Now here she was, the third speaker on the second morning of the Non-Proliferation review conference in New York.

The first woman to become foreign minister of a South Asian country, Dipu Moni is a formidable person. A physician, public health specialist, lawyer, and teacher who was educated at Johns Hopkins University, Dhaka Medical College, and the University of London, Dr. Moni was Secretary for Women's Affairs for the Bangladesh Awami League, historically Bangladesh's largest political party. She comes from a politically active family and her father, M. A. Wadud, was known for his opposition to successive military governments spanning four decades. She and her husband, Tawfique Nawaz, have two adult children, both accomplished musicians. Dr. Moni went into politics believing that the vast untapped human and material resources of Bangladesh had been submerged by the country's previous military regimes. She is deeply committed to the public delivery of health, education, and social services to women, children, minorities, and the disabled. Grey-haired and mild-mannered, she appears to have a streak of steel in her. Watching her, I was reminded of a conversation I once had with a fellow ambassador at the UN Disarmament Committee. Lamenting the lack of progress in negotiations, I remarked that perhaps what the system needed was more women diplomats to bring some humanity to our work. "Don't be silly," he responded, "they might actually do something."

Taking her place at the green podium, Dr. Moni reminded the audience that the Bangladeshi government was convinced that armaments, nuclear or conventional, were not part of the solution for attaining a secure and peaceful world. "Bangladesh views the disarmament and non-proliferation agenda from a development perspective. Our conscience cannot justify about one and a half trillion dollar expenditure a year on armament when the developing countries, particularly the least developed like Bangladesh, are struggling...We feel ashamed that the number of hungry mouths crosses one billion at the height of the contemporary technological advancement and opulence."

It was the perspective Dr. Moni brought to her address that set her apart from so many speakers from the developed countries. The starting point for the major countries is that nuclear proliferation must be stopped to improve security for all nations. The starting point for Dr. Moni was that the huge and unnecessary expenditures on arms of all kinds, especially nuclear, undermines the security of individuals, especially the poorest. Her speech was a perfect example of the clash in perspectives in the security debate today. The powerful see having sophisticated weaponry as part of the right of nations to protect themselves, no matter the cost. Opponents decry the huge expenditures on this weaponry as theft from the most vulnerable, who end up with hardly any human security. One perspective sees nuclear weapons through the prism of the needs of systems, the other through the needs of people.

I first travelled throughout Bangladesh in 1976 to do research on its development. I remember a woman thrusting her naked, emaciated baby in my face and how shaken I was. The generals were then in power, and I witnessed a two-hour parade through Dacca celebrating the power of the armed forces. The contrast between what the military sucked out of the economy and the needs of the people was startling. In 1983, I returned to Bangladesh and retraced my trip of seventeen years earlier to see how effective Canadian aid had been. Many people had undoubtedly been helped through education and health projects, but the huge increase in population and continued high military spending combined to limit development gains. I interviewed Dr. Muhammad Yunus, the internationally acclaimed originator of the Grameen Bank, which lends money to the poor with no collateral. He was awarded the 2006 Nobel Peace Prize for this pioneering work in microcredit. Through him, I met a mother and child and I visited the one-room clay dwelling with no water and no electricity that was their home. Their lives epitomized the country's continuing hardship.

Bangladesh is a land of recurrent floods, cyclones, and tidal waves that constantly impede the development process. Poverty is pervasive. The country has always depended on aid from donor countries, which is now cut back during the global financial crisis even though military budgets across the world have increased. Bangladesh valiantly tries to overcome these obstacles, and one of the chief reasons it has been able to make progress in latter years is the education of women. They are now playing an increasingly strong role, thanks to the labours of leaders like Dr. Moni.

UNTOUCHABLE MILITARY SPENDING

Often, the debate over military spending versus the needs of the poor is presented in terms of guns versus butter. The debate is thus framed in moral terms (the number of children who could be fed with the cost of one stealth fighter, for example). As Dr. Moni suggested, this is an apt approach. But concerns of social justice do not motivate government policy-makers, who start from the position that armaments have an inherent value. Applying this principle to nuclear weapons, they hold that paying great sums for nuclear deterrence is a requisite for security in a world where nuclear weapons are spreading.

As long as the idea persists that society is getting value for the money spent on the military, photos of children with distended bellies will not generate more than a little loose change. In 1990, the leaders of the world met at the UN and promised to increase budgets for children all over the world; the next year the promise was jettisoned as military budgets were cranked up to fight the first Iraq war. In 2006, the leaders of the G8 countries promised to provide antiviral vaccine to all AIDS patients in Africa; this was downgraded when they pared all but military budgets during the global financial crisis.

Whatever happens, military budgets always go up because they are deemed essential, while human development programs are treated as discretionary spending. World military spending increased 50 per cent in the past decade; spending on development programs declined. The Stockholm International Peace Research Institute commented, "Weapons and preparations for warfare remain untouchable in most austerity programs, and indeed they reveal an increasing militarization among the big powers."

The world is undoubtedly both over-armed and over-hungry, but military spending won't stop because it is so profitable. The world's 100 largest arms-producing countries increased their sales by $39 billion in 2008 to reach an annual all-time high of $385 billion. Expensive arms fairs, government subsidies, and promotion of arms exports are regular government practice. The arms trade is overwhelmingly dominated by the Western countries. Ban Ki-moon's appeal for a reversal of priorities so that money now spent on arms would be diverted to combat climate change, food production, and health and education goals fell on deaf ears.

People are infuriated by the greed and corrupt practices of the financial sector, but they are rather blasé about the corruption of the military-industrial complex because they have been conditioned to think that more and more weaponry, including nuclear bombs, will solve our security problems. Thus the government accountants shovel more money into the military machine, all the while neglecting the security needs around them. The infrastructure of society at home, the hospitals, schools, and transportation systems are all weakened because of the exaltation of military values. Nobel Peace laureate Óscar Arias, former president of Costa Rica, argues that "military spending represents the most significant perversion of world-wide priorities known today." This misappropriation of the public's money, let alone the deprivation of children, is what the guns versus butter argument should be about.

US military spending is more than that of the rest of the world put together, as we saw in Chapter 3. Yet China, projected to overtake the US and become the world's leading economic power in about two decades, accounts for only 6.6 per cent of global military spending. America's relative decline in world economic standing coincides with its excessive military outreach. It has so far spent $7.5 trillion on nuclear weapons and their delivery systems. It is not just the poor of the world who would have benefited from some of that money, but the US taxpayers would also have gained far more jobs and goods from civilian investment than from all that spending on capital-intensive weaponry.

Many US leaders, not least Obama, recognize this and would like to downsize the military, but the country's obsession with the idea that its military strength is needed to bring peace to the world constrains corrective action. The US government's idea of a military response to the economic crisis is to shift priorities from traditional heavy weaponry, such as battle tanks, aircraft carriers, and outdated fighter jets, to weapons better suited to fighting local wars, such as unmanned drone aircraft, light warships, and advanced information technology systems. The country is trapped in its own delusion that militarism equals security.

The US sticks out as a superpower, but military-industrial establishments around the world also drive expenditures in many states. During the late 1990s, the Russian reaction to the windfall from rising oil and gas prices was to greatly increase its military spending to modernize its armed forces, rather than to strengthen the country's infrastructure. As long as the US is perceived as continually building up its military superiority, Russia is unlikely to significantly reduce its nuclear arsenal.

In the United Kingdom, the top arms manufacturer, BAE Systems, has made record profits based on thriving sales of armoured fighting vehicles for use in Iraq and Afghanistan. The upgrading of the country's nuclear deterrent, the Trident missile system, has sent the defence budget soaring. In 2008, France, also modernizing its nuclear deterrent, overtook the UK in military spending, and has now opened an overseas military base, "Camp de la Paix" ("Peace Camp"), at Abu Dhabi in the United Arab Emirates. The camp was established to guard against a perceived threat to other Middle East countries from Iran and to safeguard supplies of oil through the Straits of Hormuz. (These supplies account for 40 per cent of the world's oil.) China's conventional forces and nuclear deterrent are being modernized, while its blue-water navy is being considerably expanded. India and Brazil, now playing larger roles on the world stage, have acquired submarines for their military. In Pakistan, high military spending is a given in that country's attempt to contain the spread of the Taliban, not to mention the country's longstanding rivalry with India. In the Middle East, the Israeli-Palestinian conflict is a constant boon to arms manufacturers. Latin America's projected military expenditure of $50 billion, nearly double that of 2005, has been denounced by Óscar Arias as unconscionable in a continent where 200 million people live on less than $2 a day.

States find plenty of reasons to justify their military expenditures: national security, counter-terrorism, internal instability, national prestige. Parliamentary oversight of this spending is weak and sporadic. Military spending increases because of a fear that, if it does not increase, the country concerned will become vulnerable, or more vulnerable, to attack, insurrection, terrorism, or some other form of bellicosity. The cycle of spending is continually driven by fear.

SPECTRES OF FUTURE CONFLICTS

The traditional justification for military spending, political tension, is now augmented by competition for the world's resources, particularly for the dwindling supplies of non-renewable fossil fuels and minerals needed for industrial expansion. This rising demand for resources, especially the insatiable demand for oil, to meet the needs of burgeoning populations plays into the perceived need for rising military budgets. The industrialized states are now desperate for oil, no matter how hard it is to access. The oil spill in the Gulf of Mexico in the summer of 2010 is but one example of the high risks that have become routine in oil exploration and drilling. "Drill, baby, drill," a mantra of hard-line conservatives, whose general philosophy is to grab what we need for ourselves, was only momentarily stilled by the dimensions of that tragedy.

The demand for cheap gas has always trumped environmental caution. It is already a matter of "national security" for a number of industrialized states to be able to have unimpeded access to oil. Troop levels and military expenditure in the oil-producing zones have increased. The delivery as well as the production of oil for Western markets is now safeguarded by the military.

A number of analysts foresee widespread strife over essential resources, from petroleum to water. Resource wars are looming, according to a former British defence secretary, John Reid, who, in 2006, warned that global climate change and dwindling natural resources are combining to increase the likelihood of violent conflict over land, water, and energy. Climate change, he indicated, "will make scarce resources, clean water, viable agricultural land even scarcer"—and this will "make the emergence of violent conflict more rather than less likely." His warning came soon after a 2003 report, "An Abrupt Climate Change Scenario and Its Implications for United States National Security," issued by the US Department of Defense. The report warned that global climate change will result in a substantial increase in global sea levels, intense storms and hurricanes, and continent-wide "dust bowl" effects. This could trigger pitched battles for access to food, water, habitable land, and energy supplies. In other words, future wars may be triggered by a desperate need for natural resources, rather than by conflicts over ideology, religion, or national honour.

But the future is already here, the pre-eminent environmental writer Bill McKibben states flatly in his sweeping book, *Eaarth: Making a Life on a Tough New Planet*. The polar ice caps are melting, the oceans are rising, people living in low-lying areas are preparing to move en masse, hurricanes and cyclones are becoming more powerful, water supplies in many parts of the world are dwindling, the rain forest of the Amazon is drying, the great storehouses of oil beneath the earth's crust are more empty than full. "Every one of these things is completely unprecedented in the ten thousand years of human civilization...We have traveled to a new planet, propelled on a burst of carbon dioxide." Another path-breaking analyst, Michael T. Klare, says the greatest danger posed by climate change is not just the degradation of ecosystems, "but rather the disintegration of entire human societies, producing wholesale starvation, mass migrations and recurring conflict over resources."

These spectres of future conflicts are just what the military strategists and their partners in the military-industrial complex need to keep them in business. Responding to societal dislocations with military force to protect Western interests seems natural to them. So, even as the Iraq and Afghanistan wars go on consuming vast amounts of materials, Klare says, "American strategists are increasingly looking beyond these two conflicts to envision the global combat environment of the emerging period—and the world they see is one where the struggle over vital resources, rather than ideology or balance-of-power politics, dominates the martial landscape."

As I see these forecasts unfolding, two great themes, disarmament and development, come back into focus. In 1987, as Ambassador for Disarmament, I led the Canadian delegation to the International Conference on the Relationship between Disarmament and Development. This UN conference was the culmination of a three-year study of disarmament and development issues by twenty-seven world experts headed by the formidable Swedish diplomat Inga Thorsson. Fiery and stubborn, Thorsson took a broad approach to the problem of security, defining a "dynamic triangular relationship" between disarmament, development, and security. Security for all would be enhanced by vigorously pursuing disarmament and development in their own right. "The world has a choice," Thorsson argued, "it can continue to pursue the arms race, or it can move with deliberate speed towards a more sustainable economic and political order. It cannot do both."

Today, those words take on added urgency as climate and development problems pile up as a result of insufficient funding for sustainable development around the world while military expenditures roar ahead.

Co-operative development of green technology, rather than military technology, ought to be seen as a way out of natural-resource scarcity and catastrophic climate change. Thorsson taught that as disarmament occurs, releasing funds previously spent on weaponry, investing in development projects on a massive scale will benefit the lives of increasing numbers of people. Overall security is enhanced. The Western countries, however, have always been skeptical that transferring even a portion of military spending to development needs would assure greater security, and the most aggressive of these skeptics have managed to keep the UN's documents on social development from even referring to the possibility of using a fraction of the colossal amounts of military spending for development.

A new campaign to drive home the linkage between disarmament and development has been launched by the International Peace Bureau. The Peace Bureau has a long record of involvement in peace issues. Founded in 1891, with its head office in Geneva, it is a federation of three hundred organizations in seventy countries. Over the years, thirteen of its officers have been awarded the Nobel Peace Prize (the organization itself won in 1910). Its principal priority today is a "Disarmament for Development" campaign that stresses the need for governments to build human security by a major shift in spending priorities. "As long as governments (and corporations, banks, universities and other institutions) continue to invest billions of dollars every day in the technology and organization of militarism and the defence of the state rather than the people, we are in effect robbing millions of our fellow citizens of their fundamental security. Meanwhile, the tools used by the military—notably weapons of all types—are having damaging effects on civilians and on the process of economic and social development."

The Peace Bureau sees regional conflicts driven by arms races fuelled by mutual fear and calls for greater international co-operation to diminish regional tensions and to promote sustainable economic development that can reduce the tensions flowing from poverty. It recognizes the increased threat from terrorism and calls for negotiating political grievances, cutting off the supply of arms, and economic and social development programs to stabilize regions. It sees the powerful countries arming themselves with weapons of mass destruction and calls for the discrediting of the doctrine of mutual deterrence. It sees increasing use of the military to protect natural resources for investors and calls for negotiating international legal frameworks for resource allocation similar to the UN Convention on the Law of the Sea. The concept behind Disarmament for Development is much more sophisticated than simply a demand to transfer money from the military to the development planners. It is more complicated than replacing warfare with welfare. It involves a change of thinking about the nature of security.

MOCKING THE UN CHARTER

The security of millions of people today is threatened by mass poverty and famine, genocide, ethnic conflict, and terrorism. Their personal lives are also threatened by the scourge of violence related to handguns, drugs, and crime; by unemployment or exploitative, low-paid jobs with poor conditions; by increasing rates of rape, sexual abuse, prostitution, and trafficking; and by diseases such as tuberculosis, malaria, and measles, which continue to ravage the young and the poor. These deep-rooted and interlocking threats can scarcely be addressed at all with traditional notions of national security, using military force against competing states. Military policies pay little attention to the social and political conditions within the state, little regard to popular participation and consent, and almost none whatsoever to protecting the natural environment. Governments, the fundamental purveyors of security, often fail in their obligations to ensure that the total security needs of people are properly addressed.

An integrated agenda for security, addressing the interplay of economic and social development with military defences, has been on the UN agenda for many years. In fact, at the sixtieth anniversary of the UN, in 2005, world leaders affirmed that threats to security today "recognize no national boundaries, are interlinked and must be tackled at the global, regional and national levels in accordance with the Charter and international law." Further, "peace and security, development and human rights are the pillars of the United Nations system and the foundations for collective security and well-being." The lack of implementation of these glorified statements mocks Article 26 of the UN Charter, which says the Security Council is responsible for the "maintenance of international peace and security with the least diversion for armaments of the world's human and economic resources."

The hypocrisy of the US, UK, Russia, France, and China, with their profligate spending and huge nuclear arsenals, is stunning. Following the global economic crisis of 2008, cutting debt became a new rallying cry. When the G8 leaders met in Canada in 2010, they prided themselves on providing $5 billion over the next five years to improve maternal health care. How magnanimous is $1 billion per year for these eight wealthy countries? But the principal effect of the G8 leaders' decisions, along with those taken at the later assembly of G20 leaders, was to cut hundreds of billions of dollars in public spending, to slash deficits. Their citizens will suffer cuts to public services and to such entitlements as pensions, education, and health services. Not a word was said about their huge military spending as a key factor in their deficits. Development programs suffer because of deficits, but the military does not.

One of the tests to measure how serious governments are in their protestations that they want to protect the vulnerable will be the success of the Millennium Development Goals. In 2000, building upon a decade of major UN conferences and summits, world leaders committed their nations to a new global partnership to reduce extreme poverty by setting out a series of time-bound targets —with a deadline of 2015—that have become known as the Millennium Development Goals. There are eight goals:

1. Eradicate extreme poverty and hunger by reducing by half the proportion of people living on less than a dollar a day.
2. Achieve universal primary education by ensuring that all boys and girls complete a full course of primary schooling.
3. Promote gender equality and empower women by eliminating gender disparity in primary and secondary education.
4. Reduce by two-thirds the mortality rate among children under five.
5. Reduce by three-quarters the maternal mortality rate, and achieve universal access to reproductive health.
6. Combat HIV/AIDS with universal access to treatment for victims; halt the incidence of malaria and other diseases.
7. Ensure environmental sustainability by integrating the principles of sustainable development into country policies; reduce biodiversity loss; reduce by half the number of people without safe drinking water and sanitation; achieve significant improvement in the lives of at least 100 million slum dwellers.
8. Develop a global partnership for development through an open, rule-based, predictable, and non-discriminatory trading and financial system; address the debt and other special needs of the least developed and landlocked countries.

How much would such a comprehensive program cost? The World Bank estimates that, if countries improved their policies and service delivery (a big conditionality at the outset), new costs would be between $40 and $60 billion a year. Taking the midpoint figure of $50 billion as an average, this amounts to only 3.33 per cent of annual world military expenditures. And yet, during the first ten years of the program, not half that amount was provided to the campaign. When the leaders of 140 nations gathered at the UN in 2010 to mark the first ten years, their thirty-one-page communiqué contained not a word about how development could be boosted by shifting some of the $1.5 trillion on arms to meeting the needs of the most vulnerable. They did pledge $40 billion over five years to maternal and children's health programs, but, at $8 billion per year, that's hardly commensurate with the scale of human suffering. Barely half of the 117 poorest nations are expected to meet the poverty and health targets in the specified time frame. We need to ask: Where are the voices of moral concern about spending $100 billion a year on nuclear weapons while the number of people living in extreme poverty and hunger surpasses 1 billion?

A BILLION HUNGRY PEOPLE

Nonetheless, it is remarkable that so much progress has been made with so little money. Putting the best face on the paucity of funds available, Ban Ki-moon reported that, at the two-thirds mark for the goals, a number of countries, particularly in sub-Saharan Africa, have achieved major successes in combating extreme poverty and hunger; improving school enrolment and child health; expanding access to clean water and access to HIV treatment; and controlling malaria, tuberculosis, and neglected tropical diseases. "Nevertheless," he said, "progress has been uneven and, without additional efforts, several of the Millennium Development Goals are likely to be missed in many countries. The challenges are most severe in the least developed countries, landlocked developing countries, some small island developing states, and countries that are vulnerable to natural hazards and recurring lapses into armed violence."

Using the much-cited "dollar-a-day" international poverty line revised to $1.25 a day, there were still 1.4 billion people living in extreme poverty in 2005, down from 1.8 billion in 1990. However, without China, which accounted for much of the improvement, progress is not encouraging; in fact, the number of people living in extreme poverty in countries other than China actually went up between 1990 and 2005 by about 36 million. There are still more than a billion hungry people, and more than two billion people are deficient in micronutrients; 129 million children are underweight and 195 million under age five are stunted. The number of hungry people worldwide rose from 873 million in 2004 to 1.02 billion people in 2009. The World Food Program reported that the ranks of the hungry were swelled by entirely new sectors of society, including millions of unskilled urban workers driven into poverty and hunger by the twin afflictions of the global economic crisis and persistently high food prices. The message, in brief, was stark: Many people were unable to feed themselves in 2009 not because they could not find food, but rather because they could no longer afford it.

Progress toward the employment target looks equally grim. In 2008, some 633 million workers (21.2 per cent of the workers in the world) were classed as "working poor." More than 300 million new jobs must be created before 2015 to return to pre-crisis levels of unemployment. The arms factories are not going to meet this need. The unemployment crisis is worst for the young, aged fifteen to twenty-four, reaching 14 per cent in 2009, an increase of 1.9 per cent in one year. In education, many countries have crossed the 90 per cent enrolment threshold, but inequalities still present many barriers; children from the poorest 20 per cent of households account for over 40 per cent of all out-of-school children in many developing countries.

In health, the news is mixed. Deaths among children under five years of age have been reduced from 12.5 million per year in 1990 to 8.8 million in 2008. The number of people in low- and middle-income countries receiving antiretroviral therapy for HIV increased ten-fold in five years (2003–2008). There has been significant progress in reducing deaths from measles and in controlling tuberculosis and malaria. More than 500 million people are now treated annually for one or more neglected tropical diseases. But there has been little progress in reducing maternal deaths; maternal mortality declined only marginally, from 480 deaths per 100,000 live births in 1990 to 450 in 2005. At this rate, the target of 120 deaths per 100,000 live births by 2015 cannot be achieved.

These poignant human needs cannot all be laid at the doorstep of militarism. Even a world without war would still be scarred by the greedy, for whom there can never be enough affluence. But without a doubt, expanding military expenditures by virtually all countries exacerbate human suffering and deprive the world as a whole of the production of goods and services that would go a long way to improving all peoples' human security.

Tackling the military-industrial complex is a Herculean task. That is why the UN began, a decade ago, a Global Compact program to foster business practices that align with universally accepted principles in human rights, labour, the environment, and anti-corruption. Increasing numbers of companies now see how respecting human rights is good business, can help avoid risk, and contributes to good community relations. More than eight thousand businesses participate in this corporate citizenship initiative. Ban Ki-moon wants this elevated thinking to lead to increased private investment in the developing countries. Socially responsible businesses need to grow fast to offset the big footprints of the defence contractors.

The Global Compact operates on the principle that future advances in global integration, poverty reduction, protection of the planet, and human security critically depend on our ability to collectively address the most pressing global challenges. The stakes could not be higher, given that climate change threatens the security of food, water, and energy—the interlocking resource pillars that underpin prosperity and productivity.

This enlightened thinking has not yet penetrated the councils of government, so the military-industrial complex still has its way. Albert Einstein once said that splitting the atom had changed everything except how we think. Time is running out for us to make this change. That is why 1,300 representatives of 340 non-government organizations from fifty-five countries, meeting in Mexico in 2009, appealed to governments to "redirect arms expenditure towards more productive and socially responsible alternatives that could help to diminish the world's rich-poor divide and increase security." The guns versus butter argument is being debated in more far-reaching ways than ever before.

7

RENEWABLE ENERGY, NOT NUCLEAR POWER

THE TITLE OF THE CONFERENCE SEEMED PRETENTIOUS, THOUGH WITH A SNAPPY acronym: "Summit of Honour on Atoms for Peace and Environment (SHAPE)." The invitation, asking me to speak in Seoul, South Korea, was issued on behalf of the prestigious chief sponsors, Kim Young Sam, former president of South Korea, and Mohamed ElBaradei, former director general of the International Atomic Energy Agency. Their letter said the conference was called to revitalize non-proliferation of nuclear weapons and to pursue building a multinational "environment-friendly nuclear energy paradigm."

How, I asked myself, could I be effective, speaking at a meeting primarily designed to promote South Korea's nuclear power interests? Nuclear power is one of the impediments to nuclear disarmament. The same reactors that produce energy for peaceful purposes can also be used to turn out nuclear bombs. Will the expansion of nuclear energy in the world lead to the spread of nuclear weapons and increased dangers of nuclear terrorism? My personal conflict was a reflection of the contradictions posed by nuclear power.

South Korea, which already has twenty nuclear reactors providing 40 per cent of the country's electricity, is building five new ones. It is moving heavily into the nuclear export business. Early in 2010, the South Korean Ministry of Knowledge Economy, having sold four modern nuclear reactors to the United Arab Emirates, publicized its aim of exporting eighty reactors, worth $400 billion, by 2030. This would make South Korea the third-largest supplier of nuclear technology, after the US and France. "Nuclear-power-related business will be the most profitable market after automobiles, semiconductors and shipbuilding," a ministry spokesperson said. "We will promote the industry as a major export business." The surging demand for power in a world demanding more and more goods and services for the expected nine billion people has put a spotlight on nuclear energy.

Since I came to the conclusion that those in the nuclear power business should be in the forefront of the movement to abolish nuclear weapons, thereby ensuring that nuclear energy is never used for bombs, I flew to South Korea for the conference. South Korean hospitality was at its best. A guide and chauffeur picked me up at the airport and made sure I was safely ensconced in the Grand InterContinental Hotel, a five-star palace overlooking a broad avenue of seven lanes of traffic going in one direction and seven in the opposite. Greater Seoul contains 24.5 million people, making it the second-largest metropolitan area in the world. As I looked down on the maze of cars from my window, gridlock seemed to be the way of life.

My host, Il Soon Hwang, one of the organizers, had asked me to give a lecture to political science students at Seoul National University, and the next morning a car brought me to the main campus at Gwanak, on the edge of the city. I titled my lecture, "Why Nuclear Disarmament Is Imperative," a topic the students, judging by their questions, found novel. A number of them came up to me afterwards to thank me for presenting this perspective.

The formality and lavishness of the SHAPE conference was supported by generous funding from the nuclear power industry, which had provided the conference organizers with ten times their funding goal. An impressive display of South Korean executives was on hand to greet the prime minister, Chung Un-chan. ElBaradei got right to the point. Demand for global energy is growing inexorably, just as the world's reserves of fossil fuels are being depleted and global warming has become foreboding. Most of the thirty-one countries already using nuclear energy are expanding their output, and a dozen more are actively preparing nuclear programs. Growing mastery of the production of nuclear fuels is blurring the distinction between nuclear weapons states and nuclear-weapons-capable states. Thus the production of new nuclear materials should be put under international control, guaranteeing that countries coming on stream will not be able to divert materials to bomb production.

The line between the ability to produce nuclear power and the ability to produce nuclear weapons is perilously thin. Both require fissile materials, and some of the technology used to produce or purify fissile material for a nuclear power plant can also be applied to producing nuclear weapons. Use of the main fissile materials in nuclear reactions, enriched uranium and plutonium, is spreading. For example, uranium enrichment is at the centre of the US-Iranian dispute. Iran claims it is pursuing commercial nuclear power, but the US believes it will convert this ability into making nuclear weapons. As the ability to enrich uranium for commercial power purposes spreads into many more countries, the risk that more countries will consequentially acquire the ability to produce nuclear weapons grows. The world is left with a deepening problem: once a country can produce nuclear power, it can then develop nuclear weapons.

ElBaradei's program, known as "multilateralization of the nuclear fuel cycle," tries to skirt this problem by providing access to nuclear fuels at market rates to countries that want it. He foresees a day when all existing enrichment and reprocessing facilities would be converted from national to multinational operations. This would be a giant step from the nationalism and commercial interests that drive the field today. It would require new forms of global co-operation, starting with the nuclear weapons states showing that they take their nuclear disarmament responsibilities seriously before new regulations are imposed on the non-nuclear.

South Korean speakers emphasized that nuclear safety and nuclear disarmament should move forward in tandem. This encouraged me, and when Il Soon Hwang showed me a draft of the final statement from the conference, I suggested an addition, calling for all states to include in the forthcoming Non-Proliferation Treaty review conference a commitment to begin preparatory work on a convention or framework of instruments for sustainable and verifiable global elimination of nuclear weapons. The conference managers accepted the addition, and the co-presidents, Kim Young Sam and Mohamed ElBaradei, signed a statement including this request. The statement also said the conference participants "recognize significant potential benefits in a holistic approach encompassing denuclearization, multilateral co-operation on security and technology, and non-proliferation education for paving ways to the world free of nuclear weapons." Though the conference succeeded in establishing SHAPE as a new force working to ensure that peaceful use of nuclear energy is strengthened, the Final Statement also emphasized nuclear disarmament as a prerequisite: "The world is at a crossroads: Eliminate all nuclear weapons or see more nuclear weapons states endangering humanity. The choice is clear: all declared or undeclared nuclear weapons states must give up those inhumane weapons of mass destruction and make the world safe for future generations."

THE RISKS OF NUCLEAR POWER

I left the conference satisfied, for the moment, that nuclear energy advocates and nuclear weapons abolitionists can work constructively together. But this collaboration leaves unanswered the question whether the elimination of nuclear weapons will ever be possible as long as states rely on nuclear power for their energy needs. That central question raises more immediate issues, such as the safety of nuclear power and the wisdom of putting more and more eggs in the nuclear basket when renewable energy sources, principally solar and wind, are coming on stream faster than previously expected. For good reasons, the efficacy of nuclear power is questioned by far more critics than just the nuclear abolitionists: hard-headed bankers, for instance, who won't put a dollar into nuclear enterprises because of their exorbitant costs. ElBaradei recognizes these discordances. He concluded his Seoul speech by saying, "Multilateral approaches are a cornerstone of our efforts to maximize the benefits of nuclear energy and minimize its risks."

Defenders tout the benefits. In addition to providing about 14 per cent of the world's electricity with almost no greenhouse gas emissions, nuclear science helps to diagnose and cure cancer, provides higher-yielding, disease-resistant crops, and improves water management and environmental monitoring.

An opposite view holds that nuclear energy creates a legacy of serious and long lasting environmental and health problems. The 1986 accident at Chernobyl released three hundred times the radiation let loose by the Hiroshima bomb and contaminated adjoining countries; the Chernobyl death toll to 2004 from cancer-related diseases in the surrounding area was estimated at 985,000. In addition to health hazards, the problem of storing radioactive waste safely for up to 250,000 years is overwhelming. There is no practical way of doing it. And, as the Iran case illustrates, some nations are suspected of using their new interest in developing nuclear energy as a ploy to develop a bomb. ElBaradei tempers his interest in nuclear expansion with the warning: "The greatest threat the world faces today…is that extremists could get hold of nuclear or radioactive materials."

The defenders of nuclear power appear to be winning the argument, as South Korea would attest. China and Russia are investing heavily in nuclear reactors. Yukiya Amano, a Japanese diplomat and ElBaradei's successor as director general of the IAEA, told the Non-Proliferation Treaty review conference that he expects between ten and twenty-five countries will bring their first nuclear power plants online by 2030. This is why the industry now claims that a "nuclear renaissance" is taking place.

As if the debate over the efficacy of nuclear power were not enough, experts do not even agree that a "renaissance" is actually occurring. The 435 nuclear reactors operating around the world in 2010 were nine less than in 2002. The US has not opened a new nuclear power plant since 1973. *The World Nuclear Industry Status Report* holds that the relative significance of nuclear power in the global energy balance is declining, with twenty-seven of the thirty-one countries now operating nuclear power plants not currently increasing the nuclear share in their power grids. Considering how many aging nuclear reactors will have to be replaced, it is estimated that a new reactor would have to be opened every nineteen days between 2015 and 2025 just to keep nuclear power at its present proportion of world energy—an unlikely achievement.

Like oil and gas, uranium, the essential ingredient of nuclear fuel, is a finite resource. Some experts think uranium reserves will be used up in sixty-five years. Even assuming that they last longer, the day will come when finite energy resources will be used up and the world will have no choice but to fully utilize what is now staring us in the face: renewable energy from the sun, wind, and tides. However, the governing forces of our society have never been noted for their perspicacity, and so for as far as we can see into the future we're going to go on burning up the atmosphere with carbon dioxide emissions and risking radiation poisoning from a nuclear explosion because there's plenty of money still to be made from the exploitation of the earth. Moreover, the Non-Proliferation Treaty specifies the "inalienable right" of states to access nuclear energy and the technology to develop it. The developing countries are in no mood to surrender what they claim is their right to nuclear energy, and supinely watch the developed countries further widen the gulf between rich and poor.

Nuclear power is dangerous, expensive, and not the answer to global warming; but, short of another nuclear accident that could erode all public support, it will continue to be developed. It is protected by law. It is not subject to the same kind of campaigns that would ban nuclear weapons. The purpose of nuclear weapons is to render massive, unspeakable destruction. Nuclear weapons are inherently evil. The purpose of the peaceful use of nuclear energy is to serve the needs of people. This is good, or at least sufficiently good as to defy any rationale for outright banning. Alcohol, misused, will kill, but that is not a sufficient reason to ban it.

Opponents of nuclear power insist it is not just its misuse—its conversion into bombs—that provides a reason to ban it. Even the regular use of nuclear power carries many risks of radiation poisoning and other harmful effects, such as misappropriation of water that is otherwise needed by expanding populations. In a world in which the major governments refuse to ban that which would blatantly destroy civilizations, what hope is there they will ban a source of energy that will keep industrialism growing? None. The best that can be hoped for is a tightening of all regulations governing the transfer of nuclear materials or technology.

LOCKING DOWN NUCLEAR MATERIALS

This is a point that I have wrestled with for decades. Some of my colleagues argue that the abolition of nuclear weapons is impossible as long as nuclear power exists, and therefore we must link opposition to nuclear power to our opposition to nuclear weapons. But others, myself included, hold that that linkage weakens the campaign against nuclear weapons, which are an urgent threat to humanity. So I have chosen to make the abolition of nuclear weapons a central priority and, in the process, to tighten the regulations concerning the peaceful use of nuclear energy. This work, too, is urgent, because there is already enough nuclear fuel in dozens of nations to make another 120,000 nuclear bombs.

Nuclear thievery is not just possible, it's happening. Some of the world's estimated 2,100 tons of plutonium and highly enriched uranium (HEU) are kept in poorly guarded buildings, and there have been eighteen known attempted thefts since 1993. Matthew Bunn, a Harvard professor and former White House adviser in the Office of Science and Technology Policy, says the al-Qaeda terrorist network has made repeated attempts to buy stolen nuclear material in order to make a nuclear bomb. They have tried to recruit nuclear weapons scientists, including two extremist Pakistani scientists who met with Osama bin Laden shortly before the 9/11 attacks to discuss nuclear weapons. "Nuclear terrorism," he says, "remains a real and urgent threat. The way to respond is through international co-operation, not confrontation and war."

Responding to these new threats, the UN Security Council, in 2004, adopted Resolution 1540, binding all states to enforce measures aimed at preventing non-state actors from acquiring nuclear, biological, or chemical weapons and their means of delivery. However, the resolution requires complex implementation mechanisms that reduce confidence in its effectiveness. When President Obama convened the Security Council in 2009 to tighten up the non-proliferation regime, Resolution 1887 was unanimously adopted. While that resolution called for the enforcement of strict controls on nuclear material to prevent it from falling into dangerous hands, it also underlined the right of states to pursue peaceful nuclear energy under IAEA supervision. All it could do was urge states to curb the export of nuclear-related material to countries that had terminated their compliance with Agency safeguards agreements. Since less than half the world's governments have signed onto a tougher IAEA inspection program known as the "Additional Protocol," the checkpoints on nuclear materials are full of holes. Amano, a consummate diplomat, commented dryly: "The additional information and broader access for IAEA inspectors provided for in the Additional Protocol are essential for the IAEA to obtain a much fuller picture of existing and planned nuclear programs and nuclear-material holdings of states with comprehensive safeguards agreements." Translation: don't look to the International Atomic Energy Agency to guarantee the security of nuclear materials without the co-operation of all governments.

This perilous state of affairs prompted Obama to convene the Washington summit on nuclear security in April 2010. There, forty-seven heads of government, including those of India, Pakistan, and Israel, where the fear of terrorism is constant, pledged to prevent the theft of fissile material by securing stockpiles within four years. At least, the chances are now better that many states, where civilian nuclear sites lack even standard military protections like barbed wire and checkpoints, will invest in fuel vaults, motion detectors, and central alarms. The leaders apparently left the summit with a new resolve to beef up the thirty-year-old Convention on the Physical Protection of Nuclear Material to tighten security measures around the world.

Obama may have bought the world some time to fend off a nuclear catastrophe, but with nuclear power plants coming on line in many countries the risk of nuclear terrorism is going up, not down. Fortunately, Obama recognized that the summit was only "one part of a broader, comprehensive agenda that the United States is pursuing—including reducing our nuclear arsenal and stopping the spread of nuclear weapons—an agenda that will bring us closer to our ultimate goal of a world without nuclear weapons." As we have seen, Obama will have great difficulty reaching this goal. At least he is prodding his fellow leaders to recognize that the nuclear risk is not confined to terrorism. The full risk consists of a growing number of nations' refining nuclear fuels in the belief that this will solve their development problems, despite widening the potential for the proliferation of nuclear weapons. The only way to assure the world that nuclear energy will not be diverted to bombs is to lock down the materials under international enforcement.

A central storage place for nuclear fuels is now urgent, one that would be managed by consumers and suppliers as equal partners, with built-in assurances that the host country of a multinational facility could not divert material for its own use. A robust system of verification should be in place. A set of non-political criteria, including fair pricing structures, would determine who gets the fuel. For all this to work, ElBaradei emphasizes, the nuclear weapons states must fulfill the unequivocal undertaking they have given "to accomplish the total elimination of their nuclear arsenals." A "new nuclear order" is essential, confirming the symbiotic relationship between nuclear non-proliferation and nuclear disarmament.

Russia took a step toward pooling nuclear fuels by setting up, in 2010, a reserve of 120 tonnes of low-enriched uranium for sale under international supervision to states with supply problems. Also, the 2010 Non-Proliferation Treaty review conference called for more discussion of "the possibilities to create voluntary multilateral mechanisms for assurance of nuclear fuel supply...without affecting the rights of states parties to develop nuclear energy." The Nuclear Threat Initiative, a private body founded by former US Senator Sam Nunn and Ted Turner, the philanthropist, and a sister organization, the World Institute for Nuclear Security, work to reduce the threat of nuclear theft. Government authorities and experts are certainly conscious that action is needed to stave off a catastrophe. But a comprehensive, properly funded program assuring full-fledged sharing of access to the power of the atom, which would lift up the world to a new level of civilization, does not appear to be on the horizon.

Governments still guard their national prerogatives. Obama as a candidate said he was not a nuclear energy proponent because "nuclear power has a host of problems that have not been solved." Obama as president set out to build "a new generation of safe, clean nuclear power plants in this country" and announced additional federal loan guarantees of $8.3 billion for the purpose. The Obama administration is investing in the development of renewable energy as well, but the signals he has sent— more nuclear power and more offshore drilling for oil—do not suggest that equitable partnerships for the global sharing of energy are a priority.

Whether the global nuclear future will bring prosperity or destruction is impossible to predict. There are too many factors to take into account: the effectiveness of safeguards and an array of new safety measures, the degree of corruption and stability of governments in the new nuclear power states, the ingenuity of terrorists. All that can be said with certainty is that civilian nuclear power systems remain vulnerable to sabotage, theft, and destruction in a conventional war. The 9/11 aircraft hijackers initially considered crashing a jumbo jet into a nuclear power plant. In Toronto, an Islamic fundamentalist group allegedly planned a truck bomb attack against a nuclear power plant in Ontario.

While it is true that international norms to strengthen protection against nuclear accidents and terrorism are improving, the necessary legal authority and resources to head off clandestine activity are inadequate. The link between nuclear power and nuclear weapons can be broken only when nuclear weapons are delegitimized. The nuclear-weapons states are in no hurry to take this definitive step. In holding onto their nuclear arsenals while trying to build up new safety measures against a nuclear explosion, the nuclear-weapons states are trying to have their cake and eat it, too. The greed sustained by technological superiority has put the world in high-risk peril. It is an unacceptable risk.

RENEWABLE ENERGY'S SPECTACULAR RESULTS

Global warming has moved beyond "risk"; it is actually happening. For perhaps ten thousand years, the planet had roughly 275 parts per million CO_2 in the atmosphere. Since the Industrial Revolution, that has been increasing more than two parts per million annually and, currently, the planet has nearly 390 parts per million. As a result, the ice caps are melting, the seas are rising, and weather patterns are disrupted everywhere. Continued expansion of carbon dioxide in the atmosphere, perhaps to 450 or 500 parts per million, will doom life on the planet. All this is known. Somehow, the world must lower the level to 350 parts per million. This goal inspired the creation of yet another organization, 350.org, originated by the environmentalist Bill McKibben. This international grassroots movement pushes governments to act on the indisputable latest climate science. And that science leads directly to renewable energy.

If there were no alternative to buttressing energy supplies with nuclear power, there might be at least a pragmatic reason to rush ahead with new nuclear reactors. But renewable energy sources—the sun, wind, tides, and biofuels—have all shown spectacular results in starting to meet increased energy needs.

Sustainable energy has three great attributes: it is inexhaustible and can satisfy 100 per cent of the world's energy needs; the technology for harnessing its abundance is available now; and energy from the wind and sun can now be stored for use on days the sun isn't shining or the winds aren't blowing. Every thirty minutes, enough of the sun's energy reaches the earth's surface to meet global energy demand for an entire year without producing greenhouse gases. Wind has the potential to satisfy the world's electricity needs forty times over, and could meet all global energy demand five times over. The early development of renewable energy technologies is producing dramatic results. Millions of homes now heat water through rooftop solar collectors.

The overall percentage of renewable energy in the world's electricity grids may still be low, but it is growing fast and investment is booming. The global investment in alternative energy projects in 2008 was four times the level in 2004. Wind energy is already more economical than nuclear power. The evidence of the benefits of new thinking on energy is starting to mount. In 2009, renewable energy (biofuels, biomass, geothermal, hydroelectric, solar, wind) provided 10.5 per cent of domestic US energy production. A 2007 study done by the Nuclear Policy Research Institute and the Institute for Energy and Environmental Research showed that a zero-CO_2 US economy could be achieved within the next thirty to fifty years without the use of nuclear power by using a mix of advanced technologies, including renewables. China is racing ahead to become the world leader in the application of clean technologies. The Union of Concerned Scientists sees integrated energy programs everywhere as a way to curb global warming: "No single solution can meet our society's future energy needs. The answer lies instead in a family of diverse energy technologies that share a common thread: they do not deplete our natural resources or destroy our environment. Renewable energy technologies tap into natural cycles and systems, turning the ever-present energy around us into usable forms."

The cost of extracting the traditional resources is mounting all the time as they become more difficult to access, whereas the technology for harnessing renewable energy is improving, which in turn is driving the price down. Hermann Scheer, the late chairman of the World Council for Renewable Energy, said it's a myth that renewable energy will not be competitive. "Prices for renewable energy are decreasing constantly."

A veteran German parliamentarian and accomplished author, Scheer was a formidable figure in the green movement. In 2002, he was hailed by *Time* magazine for having pushed laws through the Bundestag that turned Germany into a major producer of solar energy and wind power. He dedicated his career to shifting the energy basis of modern civilization from fossil and nuclear resources to renewable energy. He was the driving force in the creation of the International Renewable Energy Agency (IRENA), an intergovernmental organization promoting the adoption of renewable energy worldwide. Its mission is to provide concrete policy advice and to facilitate capacity building and technology transfer among countries. It was founded in 2009 with seventy-five charter countries and, within a year, the number grew to 145. The sudden political discovery that renewable energy has a rosy future caused governments around the world to rush to join.

The new agency is a perfect example of the right institution arriving at the right time. Interest in it exploded with the global debate over governments' failure to respond adequately to global warming and the failure of the 2009 Copenhagen conference on climate change to agree on a formula to drive down global carbon emissions. Scheer said it is a hopeless task to try to get governments to come to a consensus on maximum limits of carbon emissions, and the public shouldn't be surprised that, once more, the lobbyists for the huge petroleum countries, with their limitless capacity for blocking forward-minded legislation, won the day in Copenhagen. "Nobody can now seriously doubt that there is an urgent need to massively expand…climate protection initiatives…There is little dispute about what the most important steps are: speeding up the mobilization of renewable energies and promoting energy efficiency."

More than at any time in my public career, I feel the need to make common cause with other groups because a holistic approach to getting rid of nuclear weapons in the name of saving the planet is coming into focus. That is why I went to South Korea for the nuclear power conference. The South Korean leaders plan a repeat conference in 2012; this time, they should be joined by key leaders in the nuclear disarmament and environmental movements. The combined global climate and nuclear weapons crises are now so severe that we can't wait for governments to lead. The brutal fact is that governments, hamstrung by polarized electorates, are failing to lead. The political leadership in the major countries should be charged with dereliction of duty. Civil-society leaders who understand the gravity of the challenges facing the twenty-first century must act.

Abolition 2000, a grassroots movement dedicated to the elimination of nuclear weapons, takes a strong stand on promoting renewable energy to replace nuclear power. It argues that renewable energy and energy efficiency are the only paths to true energy security, assuring stable and reliable energy supplies and expanding energy access throughout the world. True energy security on a sound economic basis requires that we forego attempts to maximize fossil fuel extraction and stop trying to revive the nuclear industry. In this view, the market will take care of downgrading the need for nuclear power, and its eventual phase-out will clear the way for the complete elimination of nuclear weapons.

This analysis attempts to forge a path to the future, but governments are conflicted today. They are addicted to oil, scared of global warming (but not to the point of taking decisive collective action), and have begun to flirt with renewable energy as the way out of their dilemma. Abolition 2000 took them to task for their pusillanimity at the Non-Proliferation Treaty review conference: "We are deeply disturbed that the promotion of nuclear energy and the global expansion of the nuclear energy industry was given such unquestioned support at this Review Conference. Nuclear energy is fraught with health, environment, and proliferation dangers, and—dollar for dollar—nuclear power for electricity production is one of the most expensive ways to meet energy needs. We support universal participation in the International Renewable Energy Agency, providing a truly 'inalienable right' to energy from the sun, wind, and tides, a right to which no nation can be denied, and to initiate a phase-out of nuclear power for the health of the planet and future generations."

Despite the tepidity of governments, the global energy-production system seems poised on the brink of a massive shift. As it so often does, a market correction may assert itself in the years ahead as petroleum exploration gets increasingly more expensive and consumers feel the added bite of a carbon tax. Technology is already driving down the cost of renewable energy and one of the results may be the constraint of nuclear power expansion.

The prospect of a cleaner environment and a world without nuclear weapons would be greatly improved—if all this happens in time. In this case, time is not a friend. The lassitude of governments in risking the destruction of the planet either by global warming or by nuclear warfare has already brought the world to a tipping point.

PART THREE

FROM THE NUCLEAR MOUNTAIN
TO NUCLEAR ZERO

8

How a Global Ban Will Work

Nuclear disarmament conferences are not usually described as glittering. But that is the word to describe the Global Zero assembly in early February 2010 at the InterContinental Hotel, Paris, located on Rue Scribe in the fashionable ninth arrondissement near the Opera Garnier and the Louvre. Queen Noor of Jordan, former Irish president Mary Robinson, former Mexican president Ernesto Zedillo, the actor Michael Douglas, and former US secretary of state George Schultz were among the two hundred political, military, and civil-society luminaries gathered to put the finishing touches on an action plan to bring the world to zero nuclear weapons. Huge television screens were set up around the ornate conference room, the seating was in some sort of order of world prominence (so I wasn't surprised to find myself in the fourth tier), and the French cuisine was superb. The two-day conference, funded principally by Dr. Jennifer Simons, president of The Simons Foundation of Canada, was undoubtedly expensive.

Far from being content as a philanthropist, Jennifer Simons is an educator deeply committed and involved in nuclear disarmament and human-security issues. Through her academic work at Simon Fraser University in Vancouver, she has pioneered research, advocacy, and action in advancing nuclear disarmament, peace, human rights, and global co-operation. I first met her in 1989, when she wrote to me following publication of one of my books, expressing her concern at a nuclear-weapons-filled world. Working with Canada's Department of Foreign Affairs and International Trade, she initiated a disarmament education program providing annual scholarships to Canadian doctoral and master's students working on the issues of disarmament, arms control, and non-proliferation. When the Middle Powers Initiative started, I asked her to join the Executive Committee, where she brought knowledge and passion to our discussions in addition to financial support. It was not surprising that she would become a founding partner of Global Zero and take an active role in it.

Global Zero, an international non-partisan group of two hundred world leaders dedicated to achieving the elimination of nuclear weapons, was started by Bruce Blair, an earnest, studious man who learned by experience the danger the world is now living in. Blair, who earned a PhD in operations research at Yale University, frequently testifies before Congress on nuclear forces and command-control systems. In the 1970s, he served in the US air force as an ICBM Minuteman launch-control officer. His description of having his hand so close to the keys to launch a nuclear attack is harrowing. The experience has turned him into perhaps the world's leading advocate for "de-alerting" nuclear warheads. The Cold War practice by the US and Russia of each keeping about a thousand of their nuclear warheads on constant alert, meaning that they could be fired on fifteen minutes' notice upon information of an incoming attack, is far too dangerous and susceptible to accidents, Blair holds. There have been several instances of false alarms.

As president of the Washington-based World Security Institute, which promotes independent research on global affairs, he came to the conclusion that nuclear disarmament advocacy needs to be extended to communities not ordinarily associated with the subject. While the abolition of nuclear weapons is not a subject belonging to any political stripe, it is too often viewed as a "left-wing" cause. Blair set out to change that perception by forming an organization of former heads of state, foreign ministers, defence ministers, national security advisers, and top military commanders, who now realize, albeit belatedly, that the profusion of nuclear weapons has made the world far too dangerous a place.

His principal advisers include Richard Burt, former US arms control negotiator; Tony Lake, former US National Security advisor; the Russian diplomat Alexander Bessmertnykh; and the Chinese military strategist Peng Guangqian.

They have devised a four-stage plan, stretching out to 2030, to complete the dismantlement of all nuclear weapons. Blair believes that total elimination cannot happen quickly. "It will take years of technical, diplomatic, and political preparation before negotiations on an agreement for eliminating nuclear weapons can even begin—and many more years to negotiate and implement it. In short, this will be a very long and difficult process—the sooner we start down the road to zero, the sooner we may end the nuclear threat."

Actually, Global Zero would only start the negotiation of a "global zero accord" at a projected date of 2019—after two successive US-Russian treaties, the augmentation of a multilateral freeze, and cuts involving the other nuclear powers. Since Obama had so much trouble getting the first of the two planned US-Russian treaties ratified by the senate, I suggested to Blair that waiting for bilateral success before even looking at a global convention or accord might subject the process to too many vicissitudes. For this reason, Jayantha Dhanapala told the Paris meeting that Global Zero and the proposal for a Nuclear Weapons Convention should be merged to start the process of global negotiations now. Blair repeated his conviction that a legally binding ban on all nuclear weapons can be approached only through a series of intermediary steps. First, he said, "We need to inspire and move tens to hundreds of millions of people to active advocacy with our efforts, and we have a particular well-thought out strategy to do it."

For Blair, widening the circle of people committed to getting to zero by some process or other is a top priority. "We are expanding our orbit way beyond the customary arms control community with a fresh plan that appeals to a much broader range of people."

BREAKTHROUGH ON THE AGENDA

The tension between those who favour incremental steps on the way to the elimination of nuclear weapons and those who want negotiations on a global ban to start immediately is not new. When I was first appointed Canada's Ambassador for Disarmament in 1984, a major disarmament conference in Vancouver greeted me with the demand for a bold, grand design to stop the arms race. All I could offer was the assurance of the government to take practical measures "to make inch-by-inch progress." This was not what the group wanted to hear.

That fall, I represented Canada at the disarmament committee meetings at the UN, where the most controversial resolutions called on the nuclear weapons states "to agree to a freeze on nuclear weapons." There was no talk of banning existing nuclear weapons, only of ceasing the production of new ones. Since NATO at that time was deploying cruise and Pershing nuclear missiles in several European countries, the Canadian government, as a loyal member of NATO, felt obliged to oppose all freeze resolutions.

Negative votes on freeze resolutions put me in a conflicted position, which eventually led to my withdrawing from my position as the Cold War lumbered on. It took a decade for the idea of a comprehensive ban on existing, not just future, nuclear weapons to be formulated, and another decade after that for it to make it onto the international agenda.

Although the language in the Final Document of the 2010 Non-Proliferation Treaty Review Conference is weak, a breakthrough has still been made. For the first time, all states, nuclear as well as non-nuclear, have agreed to put the subject of a nuclear weapons ban on the international agenda.

The pressure of world opinion has brought us to this point. At the UN, two-thirds of all national governments have voted in favour of negotiating a Nuclear Weapons Convention. In twenty-one countries, including the five major nuclear powers, polls show that 76 per cent of people support the negotiation of a ban. The European Parliament has voted for a convention, along with a number of national parliaments. Mayors for Peace, comprising more than four thousand cities around the world, is campaigning for it. Long lists of non-governmental organizations want it. In Japan, fourteen million people signed a petition for it. The Secretary-General of the United Nations has gone out on a limb for it. There is no doubt that historical momentum is building up.

But the opposition is still strong. Nuclear weapons are about power, and governments have never given up that which they perceive as giving them strength. The powerful military-industrial complexes are still trading on a fear that has been driven into the public. There is virtually a mainstream-media blackout on the subject, which makes it all the harder to have national debates. Yet, despite these obstacles, the tide is turning. The strong opposition to a convention at the Non-Proliferation Treaty meeting by a powerful few shows that the idea is no longer ignored, but has entered the mainstream of governmental thinking. Having come this far, the promoters of a convention will not cease their efforts. The campaign has already shifted from arguing that a convention would be a good thing to figuring out how to actually start negotiations.

Advocates tried to have the Non-Proliferation Treaty meeting call for the Secretary-General to convene a conference in 2014 for this purpose, but their proposal was blocked by the powerful states. A conference to amend the Treaty has been suggested, but since India, Pakistan, and Israel, all with nuclear weapons, are not members, that is not the most propitious route. A special session of the UN General Assembly is sometimes proposed, but, with the major states voting no, it would be unlikely to get very far. Similarly, the Conference on Disarmament, a permanent body operating in Geneva, is stymied by the consensus rule. Short of mass demonstrations around the world demanding that all states convene to produce a convention, a comprehensive negotiation forum seems elusive. The most likely practicable action would be a core group of countries calling their own conference to which interested states would be invited. This work could evolve, when some momentum is achieved, into the full-scale international conference called for by numerous commissions. The crucial point is to start preparatory work now before the present window of opportunity closes.

WHEN GOVERNMENTS ACT

In 1996, Canadian Foreign Minister Lloyd Axworthy called an open-ended conference of states concerned about the humanitarian, social, and economic devastation caused by anti-personnel land mines. The "Ottawa Process," as it was called, demonstrated a willingness to step outside the normal diplomatic process and work with a group of civil-society experts. It was so successful that it produced a treaty within a year. The treaty quickly entered into force, and today 80 per cent of the world's states have ratified or acceded to the Ottawa Convention, and many of those that remain outside have adopted its norms. The chief civil-society organizer, Jody Williams, an American, won the Nobel Peace Prize for this effort, and Axworthy was also nominated.

In 2007, the government of Norway followed a similar process to build support for a ban on cluster munitions, weapons that eject clusters of bomblets with delayed explosive force. Again, within a year, a legally binding treaty was produced, prohibiting the use and stockpiling of cluster munitions "that cause unacceptable harm to civilians." The signing ceremony in Dublin was attended by 107 nations, including seven of the fourteen countries that have used cluster bombs, and seventeen of the thirty-four countries that have produced them. When Obama became president, he signed a law banning the export of cluster munitions that do not meet a certain standard. This was hailed as the start of a turnaround in US policy. Though the treaty was opposed at first by a number of countries that produce or stockpile significant amounts of cluster munitions, including the US, Russia, and China, it came into force August 1, 2010, with the required number of ratifications, and became binding international law.

Neither the land mines nor the cluster munitions negotiations produced perfect agreements. But they overcame diplomatic roadblocks, raised international norms, and forced the recalcitrant states into a "pariah" mode. A Nuclear Weapons Convention, even if it is developed and signed by a majority of states, may well be rejected by the major states at the outset, but the opinion of their own populaces, seeing how other states are moving ahead, may then becoming a determining factor in approval. The fact that China, one of the big five, has already voted at the UN for a convention and spoken out in favour at the Non-Proliferation Treaty review conference means that the nuclear weapons states do not have a united front. The United Kingdom, by beginning a program for the requisite verification work, has accepted that a convention will likely be necessary in the future. Even India and Pakistan, opponents of the Non-Proliferation Treaty, have committed themselves to participate in global negotiations. Once a convention has become a reality, pressure will mount for all states to sign. Some, however, may not sign immediately, and there may be a few holdouts for years. It should be remembered that it took several years for China and France to join the NPT, which simply started without them. The Nuclear Weapons Convention, however, would not come into effect until all the nuclear weapons states and nuclear-capable states had ratified it.

The risk of starting a disarmament process without knowing in advance its completion date is far less a risk than continuing the status quo in which a two-class nuclear world is an incentive to proliferation and heightened dangers. Non-nuclear states have not only a right but an obligation to build an international law based on safety for all humanity.

Not to exercise that right would be to surrender to the militarism that drives the policy-making processes of the nuclear states. If a national government's primary duty is to protect its own citizens, how can it rationally sit silently in the face of threats from outside its borders?

Some states say that the Ottawa Process cannot be replicated for nuclear weapons, which are an order of magnitude beyond conventional weapons. But they are too timid. A global process of law-making against weapons of mass destruction is an inescapable requisite for survival in a globalized world. Biological and chemical weapons are already globally banned. The process for nuclear, once it starts, will embolden many states that have hitherto been deferential to the major states.

NATO states particularly have been inhibited from acting to end the incoherence of maintaining their loyalty to the NATO doctrine that nuclear weapons are necessary, while still agreeing in the Non-Proliferation Treaty context to an "unequivocal undertaking" to total elimination. Already, Norway, Germany, and Belgium, all NATO members, are chafing at the alliance restrictions. They are ready to join important like-minded countries, such as Austria, Switzerland, Brazil, and Chile, which have openly called for a convention. A group of non-aligned countries, led by Costa Rica and Malaysia, have already met to start the process of building support. When significant middle-power states enter the discussions, a new compact will be in the offing. This will be a great help to Obama in overcoming the objections he hears daily from those around him in Washington.

A MODEL TREATY EXISTS

A Nuclear Weapons Convention would be a global ban: an enforceable international treaty to ban all nuclear weapons. It is not just a vision. A model treaty already exists. Shortly after the International Court of Justice rendered its 1996 Advisory Opinion that all nations have an obligation to conclude comprehensive negotiations for nuclear disarmament, a group of experts in law, science, disarmament, and negotiation began a drafting process. After a year of consultations, examining the security concerns of all states and of humanity as a whole, they submitted their model to the United Nations, and it has been circulating as a UN document ever since. The model treaty was the basis of a book, *Securing Our Survival: The Case for a Nuclear Weapons Convention.* In the foreword, Judge Christopher Weeramantry, former Vice-President of the World Court, called the logic of the model treaty "unassailable."

The model treaty begins with the words, "We the peoples of the Earth, through the states parties to this convention…" and continues with powerful preambular language affirming that the very existence of nuclear weapons "generates a climate of suspicion and fear which is antagonistic to the promotion of universal respect for and observance of human rights."

It lays down the obligations of states. "Each state party to this Convention undertakes never under any circumstances to use or threaten to use nuclear weapons." This is spelled out to ensure states will not "develop, test, produce, otherwise acquire, deploy, stockpile, retain, or transfer" nuclear materials or delivery vehicles and will not fund nuclear weapons research. Further, states would destroy the nuclear weapons they possess. Turning to the obligations of persons, the treaty would make it a crime for any person to engage in the development, testing, and production of nuclear weapons. The definitions of various nuclear materials, facilities, activities, and delivery vehicles are listed.

The model treaty specifies five time periods for full implementation. In Phase One, not later than one year after entry into force of the treaty, all states shall have declared the number and location of all nuclear materials, and ceased production of all nuclear-weapons components. In Phase Two (not more than two years after entry into force), all nuclear weapons and delivery vehicles shall be removed from deployment sites. In Phase Three (five years), the US and Russia will be permitted no more than 1,000 nuclear warheads, and the UK, France, and China no more than 100. In Phase Four (ten years), the US and Russia will bring their nuclear stockpiles down to fifty each, and the UK, France, and China down to ten each. Other nuclear weapons possessors would reduce in similar proportions. All reactors using highly enriched uranium or plutonium would be closed or converted to low-enriched uranium use. In Phase Five (fifteen years), "all nuclear weapons shall be destroyed."

All this disarmament activity would be supervised by an International Agency for the Prohibition of Nuclear Weapons established by the convention and verified by an international monitoring system composed of professional inspectors. Basic information would be gathered, prescribed disarmament steps monitored, and re-armament prevented through detection of any objects or activities indicating a nuclear weapons capability. Whistle-blowers would be encouraged. Emerging technologies, including satellite photography, better radioisotope monitoring, and real-time data communications systems provide increasing capacity for the necessary confidence-building.

Any state would have the right to request an on-site challenge inspection of any facility in another country to resolve any question of non-compliance (states would also be prevented from making unfounded inspection requests to avoid abuse). A country found in violation of the convention would be brought before the UN Security Council and appropriate economic and military sanctions imposed. If a dispute arose between two or more states, it would be referred to the International Court of Justice and its mechanisms for compulsory settlement of disputes.

The convention would enter into force 180 days after all nuclear weapons states and nuclear-weapons-capable states, along with states possessing nuclear reactors, completed the ratification process. The costs of the agency's work would be paid for by assessments of each nation in accordance with the UN scale, and the costs of destruction of weapons and verification in each state paid by the country concerned.

HOW ENFORCEMENT WOULD WORK

In many years of lecturing, I have learned that what people want most is a reason to hope for a better future. They want to believe that it is possible. As people hear about the possibility of a global ban on nuclear weapons, their interest quickens and they start to ask challenging questions. One of the questions I am frequently asked about a Nuclear Weapons Convention is, how could it be enforced? As with the biological weapons convention and the chemical weapons convention, final authority rests with the UN Security Council. The model nuclear weapons convention makes the threat or use of nuclear weapons a threat to the peace, which the Security Council is mandated by the UN Charter to enforce. Another provision makes the threat or use of nuclear weapons a crime for which individuals shall be held accountable before national courts and the International Criminal Court.

Putting the spotlight on the Security Council as policeman and judge raises the question of the composition of the Council and, of course, of the veto power held by the five permanent members—who are the five declared nuclear powers. A legitimate question to ask is: how can a Nuclear Weapons Convention be enforced if one or more of the nuclear, veto-wielding members of the Security Council blocks action? The answer lies in other significant states' convincing the major powers that it is in everyone's security interests to eliminate nuclear weapons. In signing the Non-Proliferation Treaty, the major powers have already agreed to negotiate in good faith the elimination of nuclear weapons. The new convention would make explicit what is already implicit in international law, especially when the requirements of humanitarian law are factored in. We must not delay the process of preparing the way to negotiate a convention just because of a fear that one or more of the major powers is not now in favour. The drafters of the model convention treaty believed that the nuclear powers would deem it to be in their interests to comply with international norms for security that had been subscribed to by the rest of the world.

Nor should the convention process be held up by the long-running argument that the Security Council membership and veto questions must be resolved before action is taken. This would be to hold a convention hostage to the interminable regional disputes over which countries should get permanent membership. A ban on nuclear weapons cannot await perfect political conditions.

Just as there is no perfect verification system, there can be no absolute guarantee that a state will not "break out" of a treaty. But as the nuclear infrastructure of all states is diminished in sequenced measures, assurance that the disarmament process is irreversible goes up. The potential for a state to break out and develop or re-develop a nuclear weapons program will exist as long as nuclear material exists, including material for nuclear energy programs. But the likelihood of that happening will decrease as international controls over all nuclear materials come into place. The real measurement of safety is whether the world is safer from intentional, accidental, or unauthorized use of nuclear weapons now, or whether it would be safer in a future regime established to guarantee nuclear disarmament.

It is sometimes argued that the nuclear "genie" cannot be put back in the bottle, and nuclear weapons cannot be "disinvented." Humanity will always possess the knowledge of how to destroy itself. It is true that nuclear weapons knowledge cannot be unlearned, but that knowledge can be fenced in with a global, enforceable agreement providing verified physical control of the key materials needed for making nuclear weapons. One reason for objection that opponents of nuclear disarmament use is that curbing the modernization of nuclear weapons will act as a disincentive to younger scientists, who will then switch to other fields of research and employment. If this happens, I'd say it's good. It's the opposite situation we should be worried about. As nuclear weapons states develop more sophisticated means of moving from design to production, nuclear weapons knowledge is bound to increase, making proliferation more likely.

Like the knowledge argument, the costs of the total dismantlement and destruction of nuclear weapons need to be kept in perspective. The costs for Russia and the US will certainly be in the billions of dollars. The G8's Global Partnership program makes money available to Russia for the costs of dismantlement, and the Nuclear Threat Initiative also helps alleviate the financial burden. But as large as the disarmament costs may be, the alternative of maintaining nuclear weapons would be even more costly, as it merely delays disarmament costs into the future and adds the extra costs of present maintenance.

Similarly, the costs of converting nuclear weapons production facilities into manufacturing centres for civilian goods appears daunting at first. New capital infrastructures and worker retraining programs are formidable challenges, but to duck this responsibility in the guise of preserving industrial jobs would be irresponsibility at its height. How can it be a sane policy to base economic strength on producing a product capable of destroying, among other things, the producer? Transforming the nuclear weapons industry, from the scientists in the labs to the workers on the assembly lines of delivery vehicles, will undoubtedly be difficult, and local politicians will scream that their constituents have been hurt. The model treaty takes this into account by phasing in the disarmament process.

When active work starts—as it must—on assembling all the legal, technical, and political elements of a convention, it does not matter if the existing model already submitted to the UN is used. That doubtless needs refinements. Nor is it essential, at least at the outset, that only a single convention be the focus of discussion. A framework of agreements arrived at by continuing, in parallel fashion, the ongoing work of ratifying the Comprehensive Test Ban Treaty, working on a treaty to ban the production of fissile materials, further reducing the numbers of existing nuclear weapons, and establishing an international verification agency will bring the international community together in a joint effort to achieve greater security. What is essential is that these steps be incorporated into a common effort with a visible intent to build a regime that bans all nuclear weapons.

The end goal must both define and drive the ongoing work. Working to bring all the parts into a comprehensive treaty would be a surer way of reaching the goal than relying on disparate steps that lack irreversibility. For comprehensive negotiations to take place, the political will of the nuclear powers must be raised to make them see how their own security would be improved by a global treaty. Important middle-power states can help give this assurance.

A NEW ARCHITECTURE OF SECURITY

The questions of verification, compliance, and breakout in a regime governed by a Nuclear Weapons Convention raise even deeper questions about the architecture of security for a globalized world. Does the elimination of nuclear weapons require a new era of enlightened co-operation in which nations share the resources of the planet more equitably and willingly put themselves under the jurisdiction of the International Court of Justice? Or would pragmatic acceptance of the merits of a Nuclear Weapons Convention, implemented in stages, contribute to the evolution of such international thinking? Which comes first: nuclear disarmament, or a new security architecture? The defenders of nuclear weapons answer that there are too many risks in today's world to let go of nuclear weapons. Nuclear disarmament advocates must show that the reverse is true: the continued existence of nuclear weapons is a principal detriment to building a secure world.

After the Cold War ended, some began to see the possibilities of "a new world order," where global governance would replace the old national rivalries. That moment, which was surely premature in a world of expanding nuclear arsenals, did not last long. The Cold War ended, but the ideologies that drove it persisted. The world is characterized by disorder, despite the halting steps taken to make the political, military, finance, and trading systems more efficient. Failure to agree on efficient measures to combat global warming, the spread of poverty and hunger despite the Millennium Development Goals, and the gigantic increases in military spending are all the result of world leadership's still shutting its eyes to the rising demands for true human security. This is the mentality that keeps nuclear weapons in national stockpiles.

A genuine effort to free the world of the burden of nuclear weapons is needed not only to eliminate the unacceptably high risks of nuclear destruction but to build the conditions for the international community to address the other challenges to human security successfully. Nuclear disarmament is a prerequisite to moving human civilization to a higher level. As Judge Weeramantry puts it, a Nuclear Weapons Convention is both "an SOS to the whole human race" and an initiative that takes the world to a new level where "we can all look forward to reaching that sunlit plateau of peace and justice, which has been the dream of humanity throughout the ages."

The long-range benefits are considerable, but it is the immediacy of the moment that demands our attention and action. The limited capacity of the Non-Proliferation Treaty and associated safeguards, the deceptive arms agreements that are always accompanied by enlarged modernization programs, and the retention of nuclear doctrines have all undermined the non-proliferation regime. Israel, India, Pakistan, and North Korea have joined the nuclear club, and Iran is close to achieving nuclear weapons capability. Without a comprehensive plan to get rid of all nuclear weapons, they are bound to spread further. The list of immediate dangers now includes terrorism. As we have seen, the opportunities for terrorists to acquire fissile material and fabricate a crude nuclear bomb are now alarming world leaders. A Nuclear Weapons Convention would make it very difficult for a terrorist organization to steal the materials for a nuclear bomb. It might not be impossible, but the verification systems under a convention would make it easier to discover a potential terrorist threat.

Another immediate benefit of a convention would be the strengthening of humanitarian law. At the moment, nuclear weapons defenders claim that international law, allowing for self-defence, trumps humanitarian law, which rules out indiscriminate attacks. The customary norm against the production or use of nuclear weapons that would be achieved by a convention would fortify international law to make it crystal clear that a nuclear weapon could never be used legally, in any circumstances. International law has been growing through the Geneva and Hague Conventions and the Statute for an International Criminal Court, and now needs to contain an express prohibition of nuclear weapons. The rule of law must be the basis for order in the new globalized world. The present two-class standard for nuclear weapons—they are permissible for friendly countries but not for those considered hostile—is inimical to the principle of universal justice. A law containing a self-contradiction will always be in disrepute.

The principle of one law for all, which a Nuclear Weapons Convention would underscore, bridges the ongoing debate about which comes first: non-proliferation or disarmament. These distinctions have polarized the debate. Likening the dispute to an aircraft requiring both wings to remain airborne, former UN Secretary-General Kofi Annan said, "We cannot choose between non-proliferation and disarmament. We must tackle both tasks with the urgency they demand."

INVOLVEMENT OF CIVIL SOCIETY

The holistic approach to nuclear disarmament through a Nuclear Weapons Convention has one other great, and perhaps determining, attribute: involvement of civil society. It will be states that do the negotiating and ratify the treaty, but the involvement of leading individuals and organizations in education, public policy, law, health, human rights, environmental protection, social justice, ethics, religion, and other fields will bring a deep human dimension to work that has too often in the past been dominated by bureaucrats and arcane terminology. For too long, governments have confused the public with the jargon and esoteric minutiae of faltering steps. With the public left out, the diplomatic terrain has been occupied by those who specialize in technical details but have no clear vision of how to move the world. The principal exception to this was during the 1980s when the "nuclear freeze" campaign galvanized the public because it was understandable and had a clear goal: to stop the development of nuclear weapons.

It was civil-society leaders who wrote the model convention treaty. Now that the subject is on the international agenda, the way is open for scientists, engineers, technicians, and corporations working in the nuclear field to contribute their expertise. The combined efforts of citizens and supportive non-nuclear weapons governments can lead the way in mobilizing public opinion for a global treaty.

A Nuclear Weapons Convention is attractive because it is a single-focused idea that would get rid of all nuclear weapons in a safe and secure way. It provides a legal basis for phasing in concrete steps with a visible intent to reach zero nuclear weapons in a defined time period. The public can easily understand such a clear notion. Already, activists are involved in various ways in generating public opinion for political action. In Switzerland, campaigners held a workshop on the need for a Nuclear Weapons Convention at a conference of health professionals. In Greece, doctors published opinion articles in newspapers calling on the government to get behind a convention. In the Philippines, medical students organized a festival and fashion show to promote a nuclear abolition treaty. In Syria, campaigners circulated a convention briefing paper in Arabic to peace organizations and governments in the region.

The International Campaign to Abolish Nuclear Weapons, led by the Australian branch of International Physicians for the Prevention of Nuclear War, gives ten reasons to support a Nuclear Weapons Convention:

1. There is an urgent political necessity and a window of opportunity to pursue the total abolition of nuclear weapons now.
2. A convention will reduce nuclear dangers by making it unlawful for anyone to use, deploy, produce, or proliferate nuclear weapons.

3. Nuclear abolition has the support of two-thirds of all governments and overwhelming endorsement from public opinion everywhere.

4. Work on a convention will strengthen the current non-proliferation regime while establishing the conditions for disarmament.

5. A convention will engage states that are outside the Non-Proliferation Treaty and will provide effective and non-discriminatory obligations for everyone.

6. Work on a convention will facilitate further incremental steps and bring advocates of non-proliferation and disarmament closer together.

7. It will provide legal recognition that any use of nuclear weapons would be a war crime and crime against humanity.

8. It will develop appropriate phases to enable all the nuclear weapon possessors to eliminate their existing arsenals quickly and securely.

9. It will help build trust and confidence among nations by establishing much more effective systems to verify compliance.

10. Governments negotiated conventions to outlaw other inhumane weapons—now it's time to prohibit nuclear weapons, the most inhumane of all.

For many years, nuclear disarmament has been a desultory process, doing little to stir public imagination. It has been buried in a welter of statistics and acronyms. The drive for a Nuclear Weapons Convention breaks through this torpid atmosphere. Its clarity puts energy and vigour into the process. It enables a new public campaign to be mounted to free humanity from the spectre of its own destruction.

9

The New Generation: A New Wave of Thinking

When Tim Wright was growing up in Geelong, a small city southwest of Melbourne, Australia, he began to learn about the Hiroshima devastation from his mother. "I remember thinking when I was only about eight years old," he said to me over lunch one day during the Non-Proliferation Treaty review conference, "how could the people who did this be so cruel?" He learned to speak Japanese in primary school and, when he entered his teen years, developed a commitment to nuclear disarmament. "I felt I could and should help to make a difference in getting rid of nuclear weapons." In his final year of high school, he joined the Australian branch of the United Nations Association and became involved in the broad peace movement. He entered a five-year law program at the University of Melbourne and, in 2010, at the age of twenty-four, received his law degree with honours.

Along the way, he met Dr. Tilman Ruff, one of the Australian leaders in International Physicians for the Prevention of Nuclear War. Ruff drew him into a new program, the International Campaign to Abolish Nuclear Weapons, the centrepiece of which is promotion of a Nuclear

Weapons Convention. Wright had found the outlet for his passion. He was never much interested in sports, preferring to travel to Africa and Europe to find out how people lived. The biggest influence on him was Helen Caldicott, the fiery advocate whose lecture *If You Love This Planet* was made into an Academy-Award-winning documentary film. He worked for Senator Lyn Allison, a prominent Australian advocate for nuclear disarmament, and interned in US Congressman Dennis Kucinich's office in Cleveland.

Several months before the Non-Proliferation review conference opened, Ruff sent Wright to New York to set up shop to work on a convention. Wright rented an apartment in Harlem, and found his way around Manhattan by subway. He met several diplomats and started working with non-governmental organization leaders, notably Ray Acheson and Beatrice Fihn, the editors of the nuclear disarmament reports issued by Reaching Critical Will, a highly informed program of the Women's International League for Peace and Freedom.

When I met Wright at the review conference, he had built a list of some five hundred recipients of a daily e-mail bulletin he was sending out on the progress and problems of getting a convention known. He was on a panel I appeared on, and his ability to connect with young people was evident. "I was just twelve when the mine ban treaty was negotiated," he said, "but I remember the campaign well. I visited Cambodia and Laos the year the treaty entered into force, 1999, and saw the suffering inflicted by these anti-human devices. To the public, and to me, there was an obvious humanitarian problem. But our response to nuclear weapons, on the whole, has been different. Despite the noble efforts of the hibakusha and of nuclear test victims to share their stories, to show the human horror caused by these weapons, we still perceive the nuclear problem largely as a political problem."

He appealed to the audience to change the nature of the debate from the psychically numbing details of doctrine to the "human reality" of the problem. The nuclear weapons states are lulling the public into believing that the possessors are not the problem. "Our political leaders have been too gutless to denounce US extended deterrence. If we're to win the campaign for a Nuclear Weapons Convention, we must recognize that—for most of us—the problem is in our very own backyards. And so, too, is the solution."

A tall and slender young man, Wright is very polite and obviously determined. When the review conference ended he issued a lengthy report, calling for a renewed global effort to build on the gains made "to outlaw and eliminate nuclear weapons through a comprehensive convention," and went home to Australia to plan the next phase of his work.

It used to be said when speaking of such a bright young person that he or she would be "a future leader." But Wright is a leader now. His generation is electronic-savvy and, in Wright's case, he has already built a network of followers in many parts of the world. Wright and his peers have in common two characteristics that give them enormous strength in taking on the nuclear abolition cause: they see the problem through the prism of human rights rather than of Cold War political doctrines, and their electronic skills, now including Facebook and Twitter, give them rapid organizing ability. They are modern in thought and technique.

The amount of youth activity in the nuclear disarmament field would surprise those who think that the bomb is not an issue for the new generation. A 2010 survey of 4,362 youth from their teens through their thirties in Japan, South Korea, the Philippines, New Zealand, the US, and the UK showed that 67.3 per cent of the respondents held that the use of nuclear weapons was not admissible under any circumstances and 59.1 per cent said they would feel safer if nuclear weapons were abolished. Many young people attended the Non-Proliferation Treaty review conference, participating in activities that were both boisterous and thoughtful. "I came to New York to raise my voice against the existence of nuclear weapons," said Inga Kravchik of St. Petersburg, Russia. "I'm here with an awesome team of students from all around Germany producing daily video interviews with diplomats and NGO reports for our website," said Jacob Romer of Germany.

IMBUING A HUMAN RIGHTS APPROACH

The arrival of each new generation increases the distance in time from the Hiroshima and Nagasaki cauldrons. It cannot be expected that today's youth will have nuclear horror on their minds—and most don't. The students I taught for many years at the University of Alberta considered Hiroshima and Nagasaki as blips in history—until we began to discuss the nuclear issue in all its ramifications. Information sparked their sensitivity.

Generally, throughout high school and even in colleges and universities, academic curricula barely touch nuclear disarmament, school boards and administrators considering the subject too "political" for the classroom. The result of this starvation diet is a woefully uninformed public, which, of course, seldom raises the nuclear issues with politicians. The military-industrial complex lobbyists and the corporate-dominated mainstream media ensure that the age-old dictum of peace through strength dominates coverage in the newspapers and radio and TV. Compounding the dearth of the public's knowledge is the substantial amount of money the defence establishment showers on universities for strategic studies courses, where the emphasis is on the military's prime role in security matters. In these settings, nuclear disarmament is only a fringe issue.

Considering the prevailing academic climate, in which the integrated agenda for human security is put on the sidelines, it is remarkable that so many teachers reach out for special courses to train themselves to be able to at least talk about these matters with students; and it is a reflection on their grasp of all the implications of globalization that so many students, a minority but dynamic, are finding ways to show their concern about the nuclear weapons mess they are inheriting.

These students are the beneficiaries of pioneering peace studies experts, such as Betty Reardon, founding director of the International Institute on Peace Education, who has been a great influence on my own thinking. She was one of the stars at the Hague Appeal for Peace, an international conference at The Hague in 1999, where eight thousand people gathered for a four-day jamboree of seminars, exhibits, concerts, and a general outpouring of human yearning for peace. That meeting launched one of Reardon's most prominent works, *Learning to Abolish War: Teaching Toward a Culture of Peace,* a manual opening up ways for teachers to approach environmental, ethical, gender, and values issues that are at the heart of peace education.

Reardon argues that peace studies should start from a positive approach to applying human rights to the social, economic, and political conditions necessary to build the conditions for peace. Peace education is not just about eliminating violence, necessary as that is. "Some educators teaching in the fields of conflict resolution, multiculturalism, development education, and world order studies...are now integrating human rights issues and standards into their curricula," she says. This is the perspective that today's students, awakening to the folly of seeing nuclear weapons only in terms of systems analysis, are imbuing.

More than just advocating against war, a holistic approach to peace education aims to create the knowledge, skills, and attitudes that will allow people at all ages and levels to develop the behavioural changes needed to prevent the occurrence of violent conflict, to resolve it peacefully, and to create the social conditions conducive to peace. The technique of negotiations for arms reductions is the work of specialists trained to high levels, but the work of building the societal climate that demands this as a necessary element in creating the conditions for peaceful existence belongs to everyone.

The United Nations has promoted holistic security themes for a long time. In 1978, the first special session of the General Assembly on disarmament initiated several long-term educational efforts, such as the UN Institute for Disarmament Research. The work of Betty Reardon and other experts inspired the UN disarmament committee to expand its work, and it now produces a range of user-friendly documents and websites, with an increasing number offering interactive features. At the university level, the United Nations University in Tokyo and the University for Peace in Costa Rica offer expert courses, which have doubtless inspired programs in other universities and colleges.

Peace education, despite the handicap of inadequate funding, has made a vital contribution to producing more people who understand that building a culture of peace requires changed public policies. But the critical mass of public thinking has not yet been swayed. The public still generally sees development separate from environment and human rights separate from nuclear disarmament when, actually, all these themes are interlinked by globalization into a global agenda.

Modern world conditions demand comprehensive thinking, and education systems as a whole, not just the peace variant, need to change standard curricula so that all students receive a thorough grounding in understanding the components of human security, not as a specialized subject or an option, but reflecting the very essence of their lives in a world where we are all dependent on one another.

"Peace" ought not to be an add-on, but integral to the education of a person today. In this context, nuclear weapons are seen as aberrant, an intrusion into peaceful co-existence. The world has moved from the initial shock of Hiroshima and Nagasaki; to concern about nuclear buildups; to relaxation and apathy in the belief that nuclear weapons, preferably reduced in number, are a necessary part of the system. Now, by showing the anti-human nature of these weapons at a time when the world is becoming more conscious of the full applicability of human rights, the campaign for abolition takes on a new pan-human character. To be fully human is to be anti-nuclear weapons. That message now needs to be incorporated into basic education. It is a message particularly appealing to youth.

PAN-RELIGIOUS LEADERSHIP NEEDED

In the larger view of a twenty-first century humanity, the central question is how to live together in one world. The essence of the question is the value of life. This is a challenge not only for the education system but for religions.

During the Non-Proliferation Treaty review conference, I attended a service at the Church Center, directly across from the United Nations building on First Avenue, to hear the Catholic Archbishop of Nagasaki, Mitsuaki Takami. Less is heard about Nagasaki than about Hiroshima, but Nagasaki was also devastated, by the second use of the atomic bomb on August 9, 1945. The Christian area of Nagasaki took the full force of the attack. I have often visited the city and have seen the charred statues that stand in a place of honour outside the cathedral. Archbishop Takami brought a blackened part of a statue of the Virgin Mary to New York as a graphic reminder of the effects of a nuclear weapon. During his address, he appealed to the President of the United States, the Japanese government, and world leaders "to take a courageous step toward the abolition of nuclear weapons and the realization of a world without wars."

There have been many statements by religious leaders urging restraint in nuclear buildups and some statements flatly opposing nuclear weapons. However, like education administrators looking over their field and trying to figure out exactly what to teach, religious leaders seem perplexed about how to apply their teachings of love to its antithesis, the wanton destruction of life. While they don't like the bomb, they are uncertain about the morality of the nuclear deterrence doctrine, and this hesitation to condemn outright the possession of nuclear weapons apparently gives military strategists the moral justification for deploying the weapons for "defensive" purposes.

There is no concerted religious effort, just as there is no concerted educational effort, to inform, mould, and lead people away from the enemy that would destroy them. This is strange, given the enlightenment of humanity now occurring. Both education and religion are deficient in fulfilling their responsibilities to lift up people from ignorance, bias, and the demonization that leads to war. Both education and religion are too preoccupied with their institutions, to the detriment of infusing people everywhere with the motivation to build the conditions of peace. Archbishop Desmond Tutu, the diminutive and dynamic South African churchman, stands out because he constantly speaks truth to power: "Nuclear disarmament is not an option for governments to take up or ignore. It is a moral duty owed by them to their own citizens, and to humanity as a whole. We must not await another Hiroshima or Nagasaki before finally mustering the political will to banish these weapons from global arsenals."

Some educators and some religious figures are valiant champions of an elevated humanity and put their lives on the line for their beliefs. One thinks of heroic figures, such as Father Dan Berrigan, the Jesuit anti-war protester, Thich Nhat Hahn, the Buddhist monk and peace activist, and Archbishop Óscar Romero, crusader for the poor in El Salvador, who was assassinated at his altar a day after appealing to soldiers to stop carrying out the government's repression and violation of basic human rights. But they seem to stand apart from the institutions they come out of. Their inspiration is not lost on the countless people today working for a more human world.

The wellspring of knowledge and faith does not flow out in torrents befitting the strength of core teaching, it comes out in trickles. Though the core teaching of all the world's major religions is not to do to others what we don't want done to ourselves, this unity of message has been fractured through the ages. In modern times, ecumenical and interfaith movements have grown to the extent where there is some modest collaboration between different faiths. But it would be a gross exaggeration to say that the message of love of God and love of neighbour yet permeates public policies.

Infusing a message of faith is, unfortunately, beset with traps laid when secular society revolted against the overbearing religious intrusions of the past. If religion was too dominant in the public square of former eras, then it would be banished from the public square of the present. A ritualistic blessing would be allowed, but the central ideas of public policy would be determined by what is deemed workable among competing opponents. Freedom from religion has meant, in effect, the exclusion of religion and religious voices from the policy-making processes. Margaret Somerville, director of the Centre for Medicine, Ethics and Law at McGill University, says: "This mistaken interpretation of the doctrine of separation of church and state has been used by secularists to win a victory for their values in the culture wars."

How religious leaders should find their way back into the arena of public debate is important, but even more pressing is the challenge of what they would say once they arrived. Religious leaders—Christians, Jews, and Muslims, the three great Abhramic traditions—have yet to develop a unified position against nuclear weapons. This is partly because right-to-life issues are still divisive in their own constituencies, with opponents and proponents of such issues as abortion and euthanasia contentiously divided. The prosecution of the wars in Iraq and Afghanistan sunder people of faith. With nuclear weapons, people have been conditioned for so long to believe they are a "necessary evil," that a unified voice of condemnation coupled with a united demand for a global ban seems beyond religious strength.

There are groups within the major religions, however, such as Faithful Security: The National Religious Partnership on the Nuclear Weapons Danger, dedicated to bringing together religious groups on a local level to break faith with nuclear weapons once and for all. This ambitious and pluralistic effort includes people from a wide range of faith traditions, including Jews, Protestants, Shintos, Catholics, Muslims, Hindus, Sikhs, Buddhists, and others who believe that all human life is sacred. Pax Christi International, a Catholic peace movement, has developed a core of bishops speaking out on the immorality of nuclear weapons.

The Two Futures Project, an initiative led by a rising generation of evangelicals, rallies support among American Christians for nuclear weapons abolition on the premise that, "We believe that we face two futures: a world without nuclear weapons or a world ruined by them." Tyler Wigg-Stevenson, a thirty-three-year-old Baptist minister and director of the Two Futures Project, represents a new wave of thinking that challenges the evangelical movement to stop making an idol out of national power: "We are accustomed to equating patriotism and love of country with support for the unlimited acquisition of national power."

MORALITY AT THE CORE

A clear-cut, succinct moral call to the world now needs to be heard. Religions should certainly contribute to this call, but, more importantly, they should work with secular society in finding language that is powerful and transcends denominations. A model for such panoramic language was provided by Joseph Rotblat, the 1995 Nobel Peace laureate who became a mentor to me. Rotblat, a Polish nuclear scientist working on development of the atom bomb in the Manhattan Project, quit the project because he foresaw the massive destructiveness ahead. He founded the Pugwash movement to oppose nuclear weapons and became a world leader. He died in 2005 at the age of ninety-seven.

In his last public speech, he said: "Morality is at the core of the nuclear issue: are we going to base our world on a culture of peace or on a culture of violence? Nuclear weapons are fundamentally immoral: their action is indiscriminate, affecting civilians as well as military, innocents and aggressors alike, killing people alive now and generations as yet unborn. And the consequence of their use might be to bring the human race to an end. All this makes nuclear weapons unacceptable instruments for maintaining peace in the world." That is a message that penetrates to the heart of every religion and culture because it is centred on the spirit that animates every person.

A new, post-Cold War generation has arrived on the international scene. They don't have to break out of the old ideologies that split East and West for so many years because they never experienced them. This new generation, or at least the best of it, is not hidebound to tradition, not particularly religious in the institutional sense, and impatient with the sluggish political thinking that has mired the world in the same old problems. They have broken out of the institutions that governed the thinking of their elders. Their values are conditioned by an awakening global conscience. They find politics, for the most part, an unproductive avenue to follow, though many are uncertain of how effective they can be in setting their own agendas. They have developed critical thinking, an appreciation of diversity, a concern for justice, and, most pronounced, a world awareness.

As an eighty-one-year-old myself, I find them the most interesting, hopeful generation in my lifetime. Maybe they will be the generation that finally rids the world of nuclear weapons. President Obama, forty-seven years old at the time, said that a world without nuclear weapons would not likely be reached in his lifetime. But the world is running out of time before our luck runs out and a nuclear catastrophe occurs. The new generation senses this. Their fresh energies and expanding capacities for creativity raise new hopes that Obama could be wrong.

10

WHEN THE PUBLIC REBELS

WE STOOD ON THE STAGE, OUR ARMS INTERLINKED. KEIJIRO MATSUSHIMA, AN eighty-one-year-old survivor of the Hiroshima bombing, had just told the audience at a conference in Hiroshima in July 2010 about his experience of the attack when he was sixteen. A slight, balding figure, Matsushima said he suddenly looked up from his classroom desk. "Suddenly, there was an orange and yellow flash followed by a huge explosion and intense heat wave. I jumped under my desk. There was blood all over me. I said, 'I'm going to die.'" Had he been on the other side of the room, where the ceiling collapsed on students, he would have. He crawled outside, found a friend with skin peeling away and took him to the Red Cross hospital. "The whole city was on fire. Many people crawled to the riverbank for water. I was able to find my mother. We had no place to go. The next day, disease set in and many more died."

A few minutes later, Mayor Tad Akiba called me to the stage to receive an Honorary Citizen of Hiroshima award for my work on nuclear disarmament. I immediately called Matsushima back to the stage and we embraced as I told the audience: "He is my brother. I too was sixteen when the bomb exploded. He has suffered enormously. Now I must help him to ensure that this never happens again."

My visit to Hiroshima a few days before the sixty-fifth anniversary of the August 6, 1945 bombing brought me back face-to-face with the hibakusha and, in the museum, with the terrible scenes of suffering. Once more, I saw the photos of whole blocks completely obliterated, the charred clothing, and the depictions of survivors, their burnt skin hanging from their arms and heads. A human shadow etched in stone is still visible; the victim, who had been sitting on stone steps 260 metres from the blast, burned to a crisp. In a two-kilometre radius from the centre the earth was so scorched that the city appeared to have been buried in molten lava. What made the horror even more unbearable was a huge globe in the centre of the museum showing all the places nuclear weapons are stored today, ready to inflict the same suffering all over again.

Steve Leeper, a sixty-two-year-old American fluent in Japanese brought in by Akiba to head the Hiroshima Peace Culture Foundation, escorted me through the museum. Leeper's father was a missionary and his mother an anti-Vietnam War activist. Though born in Illinois, he spent his early childhood in Japan and returned there as an adult to work as a translator and auto industry consultant. In 2002, Mayor Akiba asked him to represent the fledgling Mayors for Peace organization at the United Nations, and then appointed him as the first foreigner to oversee Hiroshima's museum and memorials. In entrusting stewardship of the symbol of Hiroshima's annihilation to a citizen of the country that dropped the bomb, Akiba made a statement about the past and the future: reconciliation is essential to find peace in the world and Hiroshima must never happen again.

Leeper's innate gentleness has helped him to be accepted by his Japanese colleagues and, perhaps more importantly, led him to find a way past the disputatious questions of Japan's imperial past with its own military cruelties—the attack on Pearl Harbor—and whether the US should have used the atom bomb. Leeper's concern is less about berating past military actions and more about preventing future horrors by the complete elimination of nuclear weapons. He says his appointment is proof that Hiroshima does not seek revenge but reconciliation. Soon, there will be no living hibakusha to give their testimony; and yet their story must not die with them. Leeper's challenge is to find new ways to make the Hiroshima experience meaningful to coming generations of the Japanese themselves and people around the world.

The visitor leaves the museum with these words inscribed on a painting of greenery:

> That autumn
> In Hiroshima where it was said
> "For seventy-five years nothing will grow"
> New buds sprouted
> In the green that came back to life
> Among the charred ruins
> People recovered
> Their living hopes and courage

Outside, in the Peace Memorial Park, I laid a wreath at the cenotaph and walked to the A-Bomb Dome, which has become the symbol of Hiroshima. Standing on the edge of the Motoyasu River, the skeletal structure is all that remains of a commercial building, propped up to remain a vivid reminder of what happened. The A-Bomb Dome has now become a universal symbol of peace.

All around the Peace Memorial Park, Hiroshima has been rebuilt into a modern city of 1.6 million people. The broad avenues and traffic jams are like those of cities everywhere. Life is fast paced. The people of Hiroshima don't go around feeling sorry for themselves. The bustling activity reminded me of my first visit nearly three decades ago, and I told the story at a reception Akiba hosted that evening. On that first visit I had toured the museum with some friends, which, by the end of the day, had thoroughly depressed us. When we returned to the hotel, a concierge told us there would be a baseball game that evening, Hiroshima vs. Tokyo. On an impulse, we took a cab to the stadium, bought baseball caps, and joined in the enthusiastic Japanese chants. The game (it ended in a tie) refreshed us. Back at the hotel, I realized we had just received a lesson in hope from the Hiroshima people. The evening had not been frivolous, but had offered us a release from the horror of the day and allowed our minds to focus on the future. Hiroshima had rebuilt itself: life went on. The people of Hiroshima have taught the world to have hope.

TIMELINES ARE NEEDED

Hope, of course, needs action to take it beyond mere aspiration. That is why the Hiroshima conference, dedicated to the total abolition of nuclear weapons by 2020, appealed to governments to start negotiations immediately for an international ban. "To this end, governments that have expressed their desire for a comprehensive legal process, in partnership with like-minded NGOs, should convene a special disarmament conference in 2011 to facilitate the start of negotiations on a nuclear weapons convention."

The major governments hate any thought of a timeline attached to nuclear disarmament, so Akiba's 2020 vision has, until now, been largely disregarded. But persistence is paying off. The world now knows that Akiba is serious and has four thousand mayors behind him. While it would be practically impossible to get to zero nuclear weapons by 2020, it is entirely feasible to achieve a convention or framework agreement by that date. "If 2020 is somehow 'premature," asks Sergio Duarte, UN High Representative for Disarmament, "when *should* the world expect nuclear disarmament to be achieved?"

At the very least, Duarte argues, the nuclear weapons states should make a non-binding political declaration of their willingness to eliminate all their nuclear weapons by an agreed year. "If nuclear disarmament is approached simply as an 'ultimate goal,' then no one should be surprised if compliance with non-proliferation commitments will one day also be viewed as only an ultimate goal." The double standard of trying to stop the spread of nuclear weapons while allowing the nuclear powers to retain theirs must stop.

The actual date on which the world reaches zero nuclear weapons—whether it is 2020 or 2030—cannot be foretold. What is critical is to start down that path now with an agreed determination to get to the end point. This is why starting negotiations now on a Nuclear Weapons Convention is so important. If a comprehensive course to elimination is not charted and only incremental, disconnected steps continue, the goal will fade from sight. Both 2020 and 2030 will come and go and the nuclear powers will simply perpetuate their modernization programs. Benchmarks with timelines are essential to keep the process moving.

A few days after the conference, Ban Ki-moon came to Hiroshima and Nagasaki, the first time a UN Secretary-General had ever visited the atomic bombing sites. He was made an Honorary Citizen of Hiroshima and gave a series of speeches that maintained the note of urgency. "Now is the time," he said, to set in motion concrete steps, such as the entry-into-force of the test ban treaty and to agree that no country would be the first to use nuclear weapons. He called the Mayors for Peace 2020 goal a "perfect vision," for it would be the seventy-fifth anniversary of the atomic bombing and an occasion to celebrate, with the hibakusha, the end of nuclear weapons. "Let us tell the world now is the time—the time to build political momentum…Everyone must be involved. Or else, everyone loses." He said he would convene a high-level meeting in New York to break the impasse at the Conference in Geneva and challenged Japan to host a regional meeting to advance his five-point plan for nuclear disarmament.

A MOVEMENT GATHERING SPEED

President Obama, Secretary-General Ban Ki-moon, Mayor Akiba, two-thirds of all national governments, countless public-interest groups comprising people old and young, of all cultures, races, and religions—all seek a nuclear-weapons-free world. The evidence that the majority of countries in the world has stopped loving the bomb and wants a global ban is mounting by the day. A worldwide movement to eliminate the means of human destruction is gathering speed. But the opponents of this movement—the nuclear weapons states—still have the upper hand because they are in positions of power. They have so perfected the art of lying that they have turned the doctrine of nuclear deterrence into gospel. A compliant mainstream media, with fewer and fewer journalists willing to expose the falsity of the nuclear weapons defence, or even willing to counter a corporate mentality that sees anti-nuclear protesters as marginal malingerers, gives support to the lagging establishment thinking.

The lobbyists for the arms industry now do more to set the tone of public opinion than the best of the media commentators, even when those commentators turn their attention from trivial pursuits to worldwide trends. Look at the Sunday morning TV talk shows on the American networks. The dominant commercials, slick productions of the arms companies, constantly convey the message that military strength is the route to good order and peace. Who wants to challenge the existence of nuclear weapons when they are part of the security system that keeps the world "safe" from aggression and terrorism?

In this environment, defence budgets become bloated and the modernization of all weaponry is presented as a necessary condition of survival in the modern world. US President Dwight Eisenhower was right when he said that every gun "steals" from the poor, but this thought, meant to uplift, is now submerged in the new age of fear of attack. The maintenance of nuclear weapons in the name of security is a sham foisted on a public confused about how to find human security in a globalized world.

The reason that Obama was welcomed as a new star on a dark night was that he projected a determination to break through the self-centredness that has crippled politics for so long. But in office, the bonds of conventional thinking, so apparent in even his high-level appointments, have constrained him. The cruelties of politics brought him, in two years, from being an international star to being a president fighting for his political life. Whether he ever had the intention of forcing the political system still holding to nuclear weapons doctrine to change, or whether he was content just to move the system along in the right direction while not appearing too radical, is a question political scientists will long debate. What is clear is that no political leader, even an Obama, seems capable of singly overcoming the power of the military-industrial complex. For his part, Ban Ki-moon, as much as he wants to see Mayor Akiba's 2020 vision come true, cannot go faster than the nuclear weapons states, which control the Security Council, will allow.

MAINTAINING CONFIDENCE

Heading home from a week at the United Nations in the fall of 2010, I chanced to meet Senator Roméo Dallaire at the Ottawa airport. Dallaire, who was appointed to the Senate the year after I retired, is famous as the Canadian general who, as a United Nations commander in Rwanda, tried to stop the genocide. Forbidding child soldiers and ending all nuclear weapons are two of the passions of his political life. I told him I was nearing completion of this book. "I hope it expresses some optimism," he said. "Yes, it does," I replied, "but it will take a new kind of leadership involving both civil society and politicians to get rid of nuclear weapons." He told me he was lecturing the next day in my home city of Edmonton to school administrators on a human approach to new leadership. I went to hear him, and for an hour he talked about the ethical, moral, and legal requirements to make our society more human. "We need leaders without fear to battle the bureaucracies that subvert change."

It will take a combination of enlightened governments, more knowledgeable parliamentarians, and the steady development of civil-society activists to build a world agenda for peace, starting with the elimination of nuclear weapons, that not even the recalcitrant elements of the military-industrial complex can counter. Nuclear disarmament is a social movement, and social movements when they mature become unstoppable. The endings of slavery, colonialism, and apartheid are all examples of social movements that, at first, were ignored by establishment thinking, then vigorously opposed, before at last becoming a basis for a new social order.

Sometimes, in the struggle to delegitimize nuclear weapons, it seems that fear is winning over hope. With the world in turmoil, with terrorism a constant threat, nuclear defenders trade on fears that without the ultimate weapon we would succumb to evil forces. It is hard to constantly mount the values of hope that an enlightened humanity can put behind it the instruments of evil that endanger all life. However, in fear versus hope, hope must win because hope in a better future is the constant that has always driven humanity forward. The worst thing that anti-nuclear-weapons campaigners could do at this moment would be to lose heart, fearing that the forces against nuclear disarmament are too powerful to overcome, that the nuclear mountain is too big to climb. The nuclear disarmament movement must maintain confidence that it is on the right side of history. The world, at least, is moving closer to the construction of a treaty that would ban all nuclear weapons. Even if another generation is required to complete this work, what counts today is that measurable and irreversible progress to this goal be achieved.

The public will support, and the media will discover the popularity of a stark new message from Hiroshima: nuclear weapons are the most inhumane, indiscriminate weapons ever invented and they are capable of destroying life on the planet. It makes no sense to keep spending money on them at the expense of the continued development of all societies. It does make sense to build a global law to ban them.

The conscience of humanity is, finally, awakening to ban this blatant evil. A spate of art, films, books, the Internet, and all forms of modern communication is inspiring growing numbers of people within all civilizations that the threat of mass killings cannot be tolerated.

The abolition of nuclear weapons is no longer just a lofty goal, a noble aspiration, an idealistic thought. It has become the irreducible essential for survival. It is the paramount human rights issue of our time. Peace is impossible as long as the threat of nuclear war hangs over our heads. A Nuclear Weapons Convention prohibiting the production as well as the use of all nuclear weapons in all circumstances is urgently needed. It will be constructed once the public rebels against the weapons that would destroy all life.

ACKNOWLEDGEMENTS

IN A LONG PUBLIC CAREER DEALING WITH NUCLEAR DISARMAMENT ISSUES, I have received the help and guidance of numerous colleagues and friends. Perhaps my greatest debt is owed to Jo Rotblat, the Polish nuclear physicist who renounced nuclear weapons and founded the Pugwash movement, which for more than half a century has opposed nuclear weapons. Rotblat was steadfast, even steely, in his determination to move the international community to a nuclear-weapons-free world. He took me under his wing and gave me the confidence to speak out. So did Bill Epstein, one of the first Canadians to work at the United Nations, who was unyielding in his fight to "suffocate" (a word he gave Prime Minister Trudeau for one of his speeches) the nuclear arms race. Neither Rotblat nor Epstein ever quit; Rotblat died at ninety-seven and Epstein at eighty-nine, so at eighty-one I figure I still have a way to go in writing and lecturing on getting rid of nuclear weapons, the greatest instruments of evil in the world. At the other end of the spectrum, I think of my grandchildren, Isabelle, Nicholas, and Cesar, to whom this book is dedicated, for I know the kind of world they will face if nuclear weapons keep spreading. They and the young people I have taught inspire me to keep going.

I am not alone in my admiration of Senator Roméo Dallaire. Everywhere I go in Canada, I meet people for whom the soldier who suffered so much in coping with the Rwanda genocide has become a hero. It is instructive that a general of his stature has developed such a passion against the existence of nuclear weapons. This is the second time Roméo has written a foreword for one of my books (*Global Conscience* [2007] was the first). I wish to express my deep appreciation for his support of my work.

My international colleagues in the Middle Powers Initiative, described in the book, have been an invaluable help to me: Jonathan Granoff, Jim Wurst, Michael Christ, Alyn Ware, David Krieger, Alice Slater, Rhianna Kreger, Aaron Tovish, Peter Weiss, Hiro Umebayashi, Tony D'Costa, Rebecca Johnson, Stine Rodmyr, Graham Kelly, Jackie Cabasso, Xanthe Hall, Colin Archer.

I owe special thanks to my Canadian colleagues: Bev Delong, Murray Thomson, Steve Staples, Jennifer Simons, Stephen and Dennice Leahey, Erika Simpson, Debbie Grisdale, Adele Buckley, Walter Dorn, Metta Spencer, Michael Byers, Robin Collins, Pierre Jasmin, Judy Berlyn, Phyllis Creighton, Fergus Watt.

Jayantha Dhanapala, former UN Under Secretary-General for Disarmament Affairs, has been a mentor for many years. Randy Rydell, senior policy adviser in the UN disarmament office, provided guidance on the themes of the book. Mark Suh, my Pugwash colleague from South Korea, has helped me. And I have received the counsel of several current and former ambassadors, among them Rolf Ekeus and Henrik Salander of Sweden, Richard Butler of Australia, Alfredo Labbe of Chile, and Paul Meyer and Christopher Westdal of Canada.

I am particularly grateful to John Burroughs, Executive Director of the Lawyers' Committee on Nuclear Policy, New York, for reading and commenting on the entire manuscript. Ernie Regehr, former Executive

Director of Project Ploughshares, read and commented on the Canadian chapter. Ruth Bertelsen, my first literary agent, has guided me through several books. I, of course, retain responsibility for any remaining errors.

Steve Davis provided valuable research, particularly for the "Selected Resources" section, which is meant to help readers who want to pursue further nuclear disarmament themes in websites, films, and books. Khalid Yaqub transposed the manuscript into a PowerPoint presentation, which I have given to audiences even before publication of the book. Bonnie Payne, my assistant for more than two decades, has once more contributed her constant competence and cheerfulness. Ronna Jevne and Sonia Sobon have helped me keep my vision clear.

I also want to express my appreciation to Jim Lorimer for his confidence in seeing the book through the stages from idea to publication. My editor, Diane Young, guided me with firmness and sensitivity; authors need the former and appreciate the latter.

I feel grateful to many other people, who inspire me in unsung ways. Friends often joke with me: "Is this your last book?" To that, I always reply elliptically: "Not until my work is done."

Douglas Roche
Edmonton, November 20, 2010

NOTES

CHAPTER 1

On June 21, 2010, Faisal Shahzad, a Pakistan-born US citizen, pleaded guilty to carrying out the failed Times Square car bombing and issued a warning that unless the US leaves Muslim lands alone, "we will be attacking US." He pleaded guilty to ten terrorism and weapons counts, and on October 5 was sentenced to life imprisonment.

The peace march on May 2, 2010 included two thousand Japanese and more than a thousand persons from Europe. A full account of the march is at http://peaceandjusticenow.org/wordpress/. Jackie Cabasso's work is on the website of Western States Legal Foundation: http://www.wslfweb.org/. I have drawn from her lecture, "Challenges to Peace and National Sovereignty—the NPT Review," given at a public hearing in Brasilia, Brazil, April 7, 2010. John Burroughs' work appears on the website of the New York-based Lawyers' Committee on Nuclear Policy: http://lcnp.org/. Many of his articles reflect on the legal requirements for nuclear disarmament. I have consulted with him many times in the preparation of his briefs for the Middle Powers Initiative, which I chaired from 1998 to 2009. There are many YouTube videos of Alyn Ware, starting with his description of his work coordinating the Parliamentarians for Nuclear Non-Proliferation and Disarmament: http://bit.ly/1ancFs

Jayantha Dhanapala, a Sri Lankan diplomat, is widely acclaimed for his presidency of the 1995 Non-Proliferation Review and Extension Conference, which he wrote about in his book *Multilateral Diplomacy and the NPT: An Insider's Account* (Geneva: UNIDIR, 2005). He wrote the foreword for my book *Beyond Hiroshima* (Toronto: Novalis, 2007). A complete record of all official meetings in the preparatory process for the 2010 Non-Proliferation Treaty review conference, and much valuable background, is found in a comprehensive document, *NPT Briefing Book*, published by the Mountbatten Centre for International Studies at the University of

Southampton, UK, in association with the James Martin Center for Non-proliferation Studies at the Monterey Institute of International Studies.

The texts of all the speeches given in the general debate at the NPT conference are carried on www.un.org/en/conf/npt/2010/. Interesting accounts of the official meeting and the many sideline events conducted by NGOs were published each day in a bulletin, *The News in Review*, published by the Reaching Critical Will project of the Women's International League for Peace and Freedom; the editors were Ray Acheson and Beatrice Fihn. The Pentagon's statement releasing figures on the US nuclear stockpile is found at: http://bit.ly/bFngOT

A hard-headed examination of nuclear disarmament issues and an agenda for global policy-makers is contained in *Eliminating Nuclear Threats*, the 2010 report of the International Commission on Nuclear Non-Proliferation and Disarmament, sponsored by the governments of Australia and Japan: http://bit.ly/6eClyI. Mayor Tadatoshi Akiba led a Mayors for Peace delegation of eighty-nine people from thirty member cities in ten countries to the NPT conference; the organization's website is: www.mayorsforpeace.org/english/index.html. The civil-society speeches, many of them highly informed, are available at the Reaching Critical Will website: www.reachingcriticalwill.org

CHAPTER 2

The NPT committee reports were edited and subsumed into a consolidated document, "President's Draft Final Declaration," May 25, 2010, which Ambassador Cabactulan had just put before a plenary meeting when I returned to the conference. It is available at: http://bit.ly/ijD5yA. Readers who wish to see the detailed changes in language, which weakened this document, should compare it to the Final Document, which Ambassador Cabactulan issued following severe criticism of his draft. The Final Document, NPT/CONF.2010/50 (Vol. D), is at http://bit.ly/dQmMbz. This publication also contains information on the organization and personnel of the conference.

The text of the 1995 NPT Resolution on the Middle East, located at http://bit.ly/h15zVe, will be the terms of reference for the 2012 conference on a Middle East zone free of nuclear weapons and other weapons of mass destruction. It continues to be a very important document. Ambassador Mohamed Shaker's three-volume study, *The Nuclear Non-Proliferation Treaty: Origin and Implementation, 1959–1979* (New York: Oceana, 1980), is the definitive work on the treaty. The new CD version of the book is available at the Egyptian Council for Foreign Affairs, http://www.ecfa-egypt.org, or the James Martin Center for Nonproliferation Studies, http://cns.miis.edu. The 1978 UN First Special Session on Disarmament's Final Document set the standard for the work of the following decades. It can be viewed at http://bit.ly/fgEig4

Secretary-General Ban Ki-moon's extraordinary letter to Ambassador Cabactulan on May 26, 2010, appealing for "flexibility" to save the conference, appears at http://bit.ly/gtg041. See Chapter 8 of this book for full treatment of the Nuclear Weapons Convention issue. In 2000, the nuclear weapons states joined the consensus on the Final Document with this pledge: "An unequivocal undertaking by the nuclear-weapon states to accomplish the total elimination of their nuclear arsenals leading to nuclear disarmament, to which all states parties are committed under Article VI." The text of the 2000 Final Document, containing the thirteen "practical steps," is found at: http://bit.ly/fS85vu. The International Atomic Energy Agency, www.iaea.org/About/index.html, calls itself the "Atoms for Peace" Agency and works in three areas: Safety and Security, Science and Technology, and Safeguards and Verification.

CHAPTER 3

President Obama's Prague speech, outlining his vision of a nuclear-weapons-free world is on the Huffington Post website: http://huff.to/Wuau. Mikhail Gorbachev's classic speech at the United Nations, December 7, 1988 is located at http://bit.ly/e6YwVW. Former Indian Prime Minister Rajiv Gandhi's Action Plan for nuclear disarmament, also given to the

UN in 1988, is at: www.ipfmlibrary.org/gan98.pdf. There is an excellent analysis of former Swedish prime minister Olof Palme's study on common security by Henry Wiseman at http://bit.ly/ibolyU

The text of President Obama's Nobel Peace Prize acceptance speech is at http://on.msnbc.com/dS4wx3. Obama's two books, *Dreams From My Father* (New York: Three Rivers, 1995, 2004), and *The Audacity of Hope* (New York, Three Rivers, 2006), are essential to understanding the president's personal background and political hopes. The biography of him, *The Bridge: The Life and Rise of Barack Obama* (New York: Knopf, 2010), by David Remnick contains a great deal of information on how he practices politics. The text of the US Nuclear Posture Review, published in April 2010, is at http://bit.ly/gkv9M9. A critical analysis of it is on the website of the Lawyers' Committee on Nuclear Policy: http://bit.ly/gIPnP8. Former US Defense Secretary James Schlesinger elaborated on his views on nuclear weapons in an interview in the *Wall Street Journal* on July 13, 2009. Former Central Intelligence Agency director James Woolsey gave his views in an op-ed in *The New York Times* for May 7, 2010. US President Dwight D. Eisenhower's speech on the "military-industrial complex" can be found at: http://bit.ly/1FL8fM

An interesting analysis of the articles in the *Wall Street Journal* by George Schultz, Henry Kissinger, William Perry, and Sam Nunn is contained in a dialogue between David Krieger and Richard Falk of the Nuclear Age Peace Foundation: http://bit.ly/hNOIRY. Military spending figures are from the 2010 Yearbook of the Stockholm International Peace Research Institute: www.sipri.org/research/armaments/milex. Greg Mello's criticism of Obama, "The Obama Disarmament Paradox," was published by the *Bulletin of the Atomic Scientists* February 4, 2010: http://bit.ly/cSOoAG. Obama's "National Security Strategy" is posted on the White House website: http://bit.ly/aZrfUd

CHAPTER 4

The most comprehensive review of Canada's possession of nuclear weapons is contained in *Canadian Nuclear Weapons* (Toronto: Dundurn, 1998) by Dr. John M. Clearwater. In describing Canada's actions in the Mulroney-Clark era, I have drawn from my memoirs, *Creative Dissent: A Politician's Struggle for Peace* (Toronto: Novalis, 2008) and from my personal files. The recommendations of the Standing Committee on Foreign Affairs and International Trade contained in its report of 1999 remain the most progressive agenda Parliament has ever produced. See: http://bit.ly/dQ6M2o. An excellent analysis of NATO's Strategic Concept of 2000 is provided by Ernie Regehr: http://bit.ly/fiEzmr. Foreign Minister Cannon's speech to the 2010 NPT Review Conference is at: http://bit.ly/gBan4p.

The Chrétien/Clark/Axworthy/Broadbent op-ed appeared in the *Globe and Mail* on March 25, 2010. The figures on Canada's defence spending are from "Canadian Military Spending 2009" by Bill Robinson, published by the Canadian Centre for Policy Alternatives. The *Embassy's* criticism of Canada's foreign policy was contained in an editorial, "Secret Policies and Bullying," June 9, 2010. Louise Fréchette's chapter, "Canada at the United Nations: A Shadow of its Former Self," is in *Canada Among Nations 2009-2010: As Others See us,* Fen Osler Hampson and Paul Heinbecker, eds. (Montreal and Kingston: McGill-Queen's University Press, 2010). The full list of the Order of Canada signers was published in the *Embassy,* April 14, 2010.

Metta Spencer's account of the Zero Nuclear Weapons forum was published in *Peace Magazine,* January 2010: http://bit.ly/dMMoFd. The report from the Ottawa seminar, "Practical Steps to Zero Nuclear Weapons," is carried on the Canadian Pugwash website: www.pugwashgroup. ca. I found *The Armageddon Factor: The Rise of Christian Nationalism in Canada,* by Marci McDonald (Toronto: Random House Canada, 2010), helpful in understanding the growing political power of the Christian right in the Harper government.

CHAPTER 5

Jakob Kellenberger's statement is at: http://bit.ly/amoXrH. I have drawn from "Zero Is the Only Option: Four Medical and Environmental Cases for Eradicating Nuclear Weapons," http://bit.ly/9qHcaa. Helpful background information on the World Court Project and analyses of the International Court of Justice's Advisory Opinion on nuclear weapons is on the website of the Lawyers' Committee for Nuclear Policy: http://lcnp.org/wcourt/. Charles J. Moxley, Jr., has written an excellent overview of nuclear weapons and the law in his book, *Nuclear Weapons and International Law in the Post Cold War World* (San Francisco: Austin & Winfield, 2000). I am grateful to Judge Mohammed Bedjaoui of Algeria for writing the foreword to my book *The Ultimate Evil* (Toronto: Lorimer, 1997). I wrote a full description of the development of the culture of peace and the human right to peace documentation in my book *The Human Right to Peace* (Toronto: Novalis, 2005). The 2010 "Barcelona Declaration on the Human Right to Peace" is available at: http://bit.ly/bSILGn

CHAPTER 6

The annual Yearbook of the Stockholm International Peace Research Institute (www.sipri.org) provides comprehensive, authoritative figures on military spending in many categories. I also drew with permission from an excellent reflection paper, "Challenging Militarism: Perspectives on Military Spending," by David Hay-Edie and Colin Archer, published by the International Peace Bureau (see IPB's Disarmament for Development website http://ipb.org/i/index.html). The US Department of Defense report, "An Abrupt Climate Change Scenario and Its Implications for United States National Security," is available at http://bit.ly/S38Sd. Bill McKibben's assessment of the climate crisis is in his book, *Eaarth: Making a Life on a Tough New Planet* (Toronto: Knopf Canada, 2010). The "Millennium Development Goals 2010 Report" provides a comprehensive survey of the progress and problems in economic and social development in the poorest countries (see www.undp.org/mdg/).

CHAPTER 7

How to manage the growth and spread of nuclear power is an immense subject. *Daedalus,* the Journal of the American Arts and Sciences, devoted two issues, Fall 2009 and Winter 2010, to the global nuclear future with the intention of influencing policy debates in both nuclear and non-nuclear countries. The articles there, by an array of experts, are valuable in studying the complexities of the nuclear problem. See http:// bit.ly/6iZSq2. The *Daedalus* office is at: 136 Irving Street, Cambridge, MA 02138, e-mail: daedalus@amacad.org. An in-depth examination of some countries' planning for, and others' rejecting, nuclear power is contained in "Reassessing the Nuclear Renaissance," by Paul Nelson in the *Bulletin of the Atomic Scientists* (July/August, 2010), http://bit.ly/ eMlMs0

A full examination of co-operative sharing of nuclear technology and fuels is contained in *Multilateralization of the Nuclear Fuel Cycle: Assessing the Existing Proposals,* a 2009 report of the United Nations Institute for Disarmament Research, available at: http://bit.ly/flirEL

The figure of 985,000 deaths from cancer-related diseases in the countries surrounding Chernobyl between 1986 and 2004 will surprise many, but it was arrived at by three Russian scientists, Dr. Alexey Yablokov, Dr. Alexey Nesterenko and Dr. Vassily Nesterenko, whose book, *Chernobyl: Consequences of the Catastrophe for People and the Environment,* was published by the New York Academy of Sciences in 2010. The information in the book was assembled from more than five thousand published articles and research findings, mostly available only within the former Soviet Union or Eastern block countries and not accessible in the West.

The International Renewable Energy Agency website, www.irena.org/, contains much information on the development of renewable energy around the world. The Abolition 2000 publication, *A Sustainable Energy Future Is Possible Now,* makes a strong case for moving world systems to sustainable energy. See http://bit.ly/h594ST. It contains information, with 180 references, on the rich potential of solar, wind, and tidal power, e.g., "Why Solar Energy?" at www.sunedison.com and "Evaluation of Global Windpower," in the Journal of Geophysical Research, Vol. 110, June 30, 2005, available through the website at http://bit.ly/ET6c3

CHAPTER 8

In April 1997, the Lawyers' Committee on Nuclear Policy/International Association of Lawyers Against Nuclear Arms, International Physicians for the Prevention of Nuclear War, and the International Network of Engineers and Scientists Against Proliferation released a Model Nuclear Weapons Convention, drafted by an international consortium of lawyers, scientists, disarmament experts, physicians, and activists. A decade later the document was updated and, in 2007, Costa Rica and Malaysia submitted an updated version to the UN. It is now circulating as UN document A/62/650. The drafters of the model treaty published a book, *Securing Our Survival: The Case for a Nuclear Weapons Convention* (International Physicians for the Prevention of Nuclear War, 66-70 Union Square, #204 Somerville, MA 02143 USA, 2007), dealing with the subject at length.

The International Campaign to Abolish Nuclear Weapons' office is at 60 Leicester St., Carlton VIC 3053, Australia, and the website is www.icanw.org/

CHAPTER 9

The youth survey was conducted by Soka Gakkai International from January to March 2010, e-mail: janderson@sgi.gr.jp. Information about how to download Betty Reardon's peace manuals can be obtained at the Hague Appeal for Peace website www.haguepeace.org/. An excellent compendium of religious views on nuclear disarmament, *The Fire Next Time: Faith and the Future of Nuclear Weapons,* was published as the Spring 2009, issue of *Reflections* by Yale Divinity School. Contact: reflections.editor@yale.edu, http://scr.bi/dFbiXC

CHAPTER 10

The complete story of the Hiroshima tragedy is contained in *The Spirit of Hiroshima,* an illustrated book in English and Japanese published by the Hiroshima Peace Memorial Museum. More information can be found at the museum's website: www.pcf.city.hiroshima.jp, in English under the "English Web Site" tab. One of the best newspaper articles that I have seen, giving a comprehensive overview of the meaning of Hiroshima to the modern world, is "Abolishing Nukes: Flicker of Hope to Global Cause," by Charles J. Hanley, the Associated Press, published August 8, 2010: http://on.msnbc.com/eLtivV

SELECTED RESOURCES

For readers wishing to delve more deeply into nuclear disarmament issues, there is a wide range of material in the websites of dynamic organizations, in films, and in books. The following is a small selection.

WEBSITES

ACRONYM INSTITUTE FOR DISARMAMENT DIPLOMACY
www.acronym.org.uk
Since 1995, Acronym has worked to promote effective approaches to international security, disarmament, and arms control. Engaging with governments and civil society, Acronym reports on issues relevant to peace and security, with a special emphasis on treaties and multilateral initiatives.

BULLETIN OF THE ATOMIC SCIENTISTS
www.thebulletin.org
Creator of the famous "Doomsday Clock," which represents the estimated risk of nuclear conflict, the *Bulletin of the Atomic Scientists* has been in operation since the creation of nuclear weapons in 1945. It deals with threats to the survival and development of humanity from nuclear weapons, climate change, and emerging technologies in the life sciences. Go online to sign up for their newsletter or to access their vast archive of articles and analysis.

DAISY ALLIANCE
www.daisyalliance.org
The Daisy Alliance is a nonpartisan grassroots peace organization seeking global security through nuclear non-proliferation, disarmament, and the elimination of nuclear, chemical, and biological weapons. The website hosts a blog, a newsletter, essay competitions, and an interview section.

GLOBAL SECURITY INSTITUTE (GSI)

www.gsinstitute.org

Created by the eminent, late Senator Alan Cranston, GSI has convened many meetings of high-level experts, officials, and other public personalities to broker progress on nuclear abolition. Under Jonathan Granoff, it has developed a dynamic network of diplomats, parliamentarians, and celebrities. The website is frequently updated with event information and suggestions about how the public can contribute to the cause.

GLOBAL ZERO

www.globalzero.org

The international Global Zero movement, launched in December 2008, includes more than two hundred political, military, business, faith, and civic leaders—and hundreds of thousands of citizens—working for the phased, verified elimination of all nuclear weapons worldwide. The website shows students how to start a chapter at their school, and offers an online declaration that anyone can sign.

INTERNATIONAL NETWORK OF ENGINEERS AND SCIENTISTS AGAINST PROLIFERATION

www.inesap.org

The reduction and elimination of nuclear weapons presents a host of complex and evolving technical and scientific challenges. This broadly qualified organization provides invaluable assistance in crafting feasible, safe, and economical solutions for nuclear disarmament.

INTERNATIONAL ASSOCIATION OF LAWYERS AGAINST NUCLEAR ARMS (IALANA)

www.ialana.net

The long-term success of the Nuclear Non-Proliferation Treaty requires legal expertise in negotiating the elimination of nuclear weapons. With international offices in Germany, Sri Lanka, the US, and New Zealand, IALANA advances peaceful, rule-based approaches to armed conflict.

INTERNATIONAL PEACE BUREAU (IPB)

www.ipb.org

Nearly 120 years old, this respected and experienced peace organization has stood the test of time. IPB serves as a hub through which thousands of local, national, and international peace organizations can pool resources, share information, and network for greater results.

INTERNATIONAL PHYSICIANS FOR THE PREVENTION OF NUCLEAR WAR (IPPNW)

www.ippnw.org

The Hippocratic oath and knowledge of human health place a special responsibility on medical doctors to prevent the spread and use of nuclear weapons. For thirty years, IPPNW has worked toward this goal, and was awarded the Nobel Peace Prize in 1985. Look in the Resources section for a 2010 publication, *Zero is the Only Option: Four Medical and Environmental Cases for Eradicating Nuclear Weapons.*

INTERNATIONAL TRADE UNION CONFEDERATION

www.ituc-csi.org/+-no-to-nuclear-weapons-+.html

Complementing the medical and scientific nuclear abolition organizations driven by technical expertise, this group works from the perspective of social justice. In July 2009, it started a petition against nuclear weapons and quickly gained the support of 6.7 million individuals.

MAYORS FOR PEACE

www.mayorsforpeace.org

Of all the nuclear abolition organizations, this is likely the one that directly touches the most lives. More than four thousand cities in 144 countries have endorsed its call for a nuclear-weapons-free world by

2020. Mayors for Peace also helps municipal officials establish nuclear-weapons-free zones.

MIDDLE POWERS INITIATIVE (MPI)
www.middlepowers.org
Eight prominent organizations advocating the elimination of nuclear weapons formed MPI in 1998 to work with key middle-power states, encouraging them to press the nuclear powers to fulfill their legal obligations to nuclear disarmament. MPI's Article VI Forum has examined the legal, political, and technical requirements for a nuclear-weapons-free world.

NATIONAL SECURITY ARCHIVE
www.nsarchive.org
A small team at George Washington University (Washington, DC) acquires and distributes some of the world's most sensitive documents for public review and scholarly analysis. This excellent site continually adds newly declassified documents concerning nuclear weapons.

NOBEL WOMEN'S INITIATIVE
www.nobelwomensinitiative.org
Six women who have won the Nobel Peace Prize—Jody Williams, Shirin Ebadi, Wangari Maathai, Rigoberta Menchú Tum, Betty Williams, and Mairead Corrigan Maguire—formed the Nobel Women's Initiative in 2006 to advance the cause of peace, justice, and equality. Look at their website to find out how to involve more women in the elimination of nuclear weapons.

NUCLEAR AGE PEACE FOUNDATION
www.wagingpeace.org
For nearly three decades, this California-based, non-partisan education and advocacy organization has initiated and supported worldwide

efforts to abolish nuclear weapons, strengthen international law and institutions, and empower a new generation of peace leaders. It is recognized by the United Nations as a Peace Messenger Organization.

PARLIAMENTARIANS FOR NUCLEAR NON-PROLIFERATION AND DISARMAMENT (PNND)

www.gsinstitute.org/pnnd/

PNND is a global network of more than seven hundred parliamentarians from over seventy-five countries working to prevent nuclear proliferation and to achieve nuclear disarmament. Membership is open to current members of legislatures and parliaments at state, federal, national, and regional levels. The website contains information in a dozen languages, making it easy for politicians from around the world to join.

PUGWASH CONFERENCES ON SCIENCE AND WORLD AFFAIRS

www.pugwash.org

Pugwash brings together influential scholars and public figures to reduce the danger of armed conflict through co-operative solutions. At annual conferences, participants exchange views and explore alternative approaches to arms control and tension reduction. The website has regional analyses, issue discussions, a newsletter, and an up-to-date list of projects and events.

REACHING CRITICAL WILL (RCW)

www.reachingcriticalwill.org

A project of the oldest women's peace organization in the world, the Women's International League for Peace and Freedom, Reaching Critical Will tracks and disseminates information about nuclear disarmament. RCW's website contains first-hand insight into international meetings and treaties.

UNITED NATIONS OFFICE FOR DISARMAMENT AFFAIRS (UNODA)

www.un.org/disarmament/

The UNODA website provides one-stop shopping for disarmament information. The site provides easy access to all resolutions and discussions regarding nuclear weapons at the UN. Viewers can search a database of resolutions, check the status of treaties, and view a calendar of events and meetings. There's also a video library with ten educational films, including *Ground Zero: Documents of Hiroshima* and *Nuclear Weapons and the Human Future.*

WESTERN STATES LEGAL FOUNDATION (WSLF)

www.wslfweb.org

WSLF is a non-profit, public-interest organization founded in 1982, which monitors and analyzes US nuclear weapons programs and policies and related high-technology energy and weapons programs, with a focus on the legal aspects of American nuclear weapons laboratories.

YOUTH WEBSITES

GLOBAL YOUTH ACTION NETWORK

www.youthlink.org

A network of twelve hundred youth-led and youth-serving organizations in 190 countries, with an outreach to ten thousand organizations, facilitates the active participation of youth in United Nations work. The full range of UN activities is covered.

BAN ALL NUKES GENERATION, EUROPEAN YOUTH NETWORK FOR NUCLEAR DISARMAMENT

www.bang-europe.org

Anyone joining the e-mail list becomes a member and can organize a non-violent action program. Its principal work is conducting debates and seminars on nuclear disarmament issues in universities.

PEACEBOAT
www.peaceboat.org/english
A Japan-based chartered passenger ship that regularly travels the world, conducting peace education programs at sea and in ports of call. It provides innovative approaches to peace and sustainability-related studies through intensive learning onboard and direct exposure to issues in various countries.

ENACT—YOUTH ENABLING ACTION
www.enact.org.nz
New Zealand-based, it engages young people in peace issues and activities, and promotes youth initiatives on non-violence, conflict resolution, and cross-cultural understanding. Students have an opportunity to talk to other people interested in peace, ask questions, share peace lessons, and showcase talent on Facebook.

In addition, International Physicians for the Prevention of Nuclear War (www.ippnw.org), the Nuclear Age Peace Foundation (www.wagingpeace. org), and Alliance of Civilizations (www.unaoc.org) devote sections to youth education and program activities on their websites. The Religions for Peace Global Youth Network (www.religionsforpeace.org/initiatives/global-youth-network/) harnesses the energy and commitment of religious youth leaders around the world to advance multi-religious co-operation for peace

FILMS

AMAZING GRACE
(Available on DVD at amazon.com.)
Although slavery may often seem like a savage practice of the distant past, it should be remembered that just two hundred years ago it was not only widely practiced but socially accepted and legally protected. There are many parallels between the campaigns to eliminate slavery

and to eliminate nuclear weapons, and this film poignantly reveals the challenges associated with resisting established practices and policies.

COUNTDOWN TO ZERO

(Go to takepart.com/countdowntozero for news and for purchase information.)

In this film, viewers are taken through the past, present, and possible future of nuclear weapons by the former leaders of the United States, Russia, the United Kingdom, and Pakistan. Oscar-winning filmmaker Lawrence Bender shows how the world's fragile nuclear balance could be shattered by an act of terrorism, failed diplomacy, or a simple accident. This controversial film has inspired heated responses from both supporters and detractors of nuclear weapons.

DR. STRANGELOVE, OR: HOW I LEARNED TO STOP WORRYING AND LOVE THE BOMB

(Available on DVD at amazon.com.)

A cinematic masterpiece by director Stanley Kubrick and starring Peter Sellers, this 1964 film takes black humour to the extreme and shows some of the assumptions and absurdity that still expose our planet to grave risk to the present day. Also worth viewing is the "making of" featurette on DVD that gives further insight into the production.

THE FOG OF WAR

(Available on DVD at amazon.com.)

If one could watch only one film illustrating the dangers associated with nuclear weapons, this should be it. As US Secretary of Defense through the Cuban missile crisis in 1962, Robert McNamara has a unique perspective on the use and nature of nuclear weapons. He poignantly confesses his own miscalculations to show how the world has averted nuclear annihilation through sheer luck, and why we must change present conflict resolution strategies.

NUCLEAR TIPPING POINT

(Order a free copy at nucleartippingpoint.org.)

George Schultz and Henry Kissinger, both former secretaries of state under Republican presidents, former Democratic senator Sam Nunn, and William J. Perry, former secretary of defense in the Clinton administration, came together to appear in a rarely seen non-partisan consensus arguing for the abolition of nuclear weapons. President Obama screened this film in the White House with Kissinger, Schultz, Perry, and Nunn in attendance.

PATHS TO ZERO

(Watch online at vimeo.com/11083574.)

In this free online short film, Dr. Ivan Oelrich, Vice-President of the Federation of American Scientists, explains how the nuclear-armed world got to this point, and how we can begin to move down a path to zero.

THE STRANGEST DREAM

(Order online at films.nfb.ca/strangest-dream.)

Produced by Canada's National Film Board, the film highlights the life of Joseph Rotblat, former scientist on the Manhattan Project and later Nobel Peace Prize winner. It is a moving exploration of how Rotblat, Bertrand Russell and other leading thinkers felt compelled to develop the modern peace movement after working on weapons of mass destruction.

THIRTEEN DAYS

(Available on DVD at amazon.com.)

This gripping dramatization of history takes people into the corridors of power to see how the American and Soviet military nearly went to war several times despite efforts to avert conflict by leaders on both sides. Through the stellar acting of Kevin Costner, we see how human relationships and simple misunderstandings can rapidly escalate to all-out war.

WHY WE FIGHT
(Available on DVD at amazon.com.)
Taking its name from a series of World War II propaganda films directed by Frank Capra, this shrewd and intelligent polemic traces the roots of the "military-industrial complex" in the United States.

BOOKS

Acheson, Ray, ed. *Beyond Arms Control: Challenges and Choices for Nuclear Disarmament.* New York: Reaching Critical Will, 2010.

The book serves as a primer on the range of issues that make up the nuclear disarmament agenda. Though written in the run-up to the 2010 review conference of the Non-Proliferation Treaty, it has continuing validity on the hot-button issues of the impact of nuclear weapons modernization, NATO, the Middle East, missile defence, and nuclear energy.

Green, Rob. *Security Without Nuclear Deterrence.* Christchurch: Astron Media and the Disarmament and Security Centre, 2010.

A former operator of British nuclear weapons, Rob Green has become a leading nuclear disarmament campaigner. His book exposes the dangerous contradictions within the nuclear deterrence doctrine and offers credible strategies to achieve real security.

International Association of Lawyers Against Nuclear Arms, International Network of Engineers and Scientists Against Proliferation, and International Physicians for the Prevention of Nuclear War. *Securing Our Survival: The Case for a Nuclear Weapons Convention.* 2007.

What is a Nuclear Weapons Convention and how can it be achieved? The answers are in this valuable guide, prepared by experts in law, science, disarmament, and negotiation. The critical questions of enforcement, security, breakout, deterrence, terrorism are explained in a very readable presentation.

Krieger, David, ed. The *Challenge of Abolishing Nuclear Weapons*. New Brunswick (USA) and London: Transaction Publishers, 2007.

Edited by the distinguished director of the Nuclear Age Peace Foundation, these thoughtful essays provide historical perspectives on nuclear weapons policies, explore the role of international law, present a path to achieving a nuclear-weapons-free world, and discuss the role of citizens in achieving such a world.

Makhijani, Arjun. *Carbon-Free and Nuclear-Free: A Roadmap for U.S. Energy Policy*. Takoma Park: IEER Press, and Muskegon: RDR Books, 2007.

Is nuclear power necessary to meet burgeoning energy needs without added carbon gases? Definitely not, says the president of the Institute for Energy and Environmental Research. He presents a roadmap to achieving a zero-CO_2 economy through energy technologies eliminating nuclear power and highlighting the mass use of renewable energy.

Rhodes, Richard. *The Twilight of the Bombs*. New York: Knopf, 2010.

The acclaimed historian of the nuclear age explains how the past two decades have transformed our understanding of nuclear weapons and brought the world to a turning point: we must decide whether to go on living with incalculable dangers or to summon up the will to move to a post-nuclear era.

Schell, Jonathan. *The Seventh Decade: The New Shape of Nuclear Danger*. New York: Henry Holt, 2007.

The renowned author of the best-seller *The Fate of the Earth* appraises the growing perils with the nuclear age now in its seventh decade. Schell argues that a dangerous dynamic is at work: the nuclear weapons possessors won't let go, and would-be proliferators are hell-bent on acquiring the bomb.

Wittner, Lawrence S. *Confronting the Bomb: A Short History of the World Nuclear Disarmament Movement.* Palo Alto: Stanford University Press, 2009.

Are the people of the world capable of responding to the nuclear weapons challenge? Yes, says the author, a historian of the peace movement. Millions of people have already joined hands to build a safer, saner world. Citizen activism has already helped to curb the nuclear arms race and prevent nuclear war.

INDEX